Secrets of the Sword

SECRETS OF
THE SWORD

BARON DE BAZANCOURT

TRANSLATED BY C. F. CLAY

ILLUSTRATIONS BY F. H. TOWNSEND

*La pointe d'une épée est une
réalité qui fait disparaître bien
des fantômes.*
BANZANCOURT.

A LANCE C. LOBO BOOK

LAUREATE PRESS
BANGOR, MAINE

Secrets of the Sword
Copyright © 1998 by Laureate Press

Laureate Press – Telephone 800-946-2727

Manufactured in the United States of America.

 The paper used in this book meets the minimum requirements of the American
National Standard for Information Services – Permanence of Paper for Printed
Library Materials, ANSI Z39.48-1984.

First Edition 2 4 6 8 10 9 7 5 3 1

Library of Congress Catalog Card Number: 98-67196

Library of Congress Cataloging in Publication Data
Bazancourt, Baron de
  Secrets of the Sword; Translated by C. F. Clay, Illustrations by F. H. Townsend
    p. cm.
  "A Lance C. Lobo Book"
  ISBN 1-884528-18-X (alk. paper) $19.95
  1. Fencing. I. Clay, C. F. II. Townsend, F. H. III. Title.
  GV1147   98-67196
  786.8'6—dc20   CIP

Warning – Disclaimer
This book is designed to provide information in regard to the subject matter
covered. It is sold with the understanding that the publisher is not engaged in
rendering advice or other services. If expert assistance is required, the services of
a competent professional should be sought. This text should be used only as a
general guide and not as the ultimate source of information on the subject.

The publisher shall have neither liability nor responsibility to any person or
entity with respect to any loss, injury, libel or damage caused, or alleged to be
caused, directly or indirectly by the information contained in this book. Opinions
expressed in this book are solely those of the author.

If you do not wish to be bound by the above, you may return this book to the
publisher for a full refund.

PREFACE

I F French is, as we have been told, the natural language of the art of fencing, it seems a particularly rash venture to translate a French book on the subject into English. This is especially the case when the original is such a work as *Les Secrets de l'Épée*, which so far from being a dry technical manual, that might be sufficiently rendered by a baldly literal version, is one of those fascinating, chatty books, written in a happy vein, in which the manner of writing is the matter of principal importance. But the delightful ease and artful simplicity of style that captivate the reader are the translator's despair. I have made the attempt for my own amusement, and I am publishing my translation because the original work, which was first published in 1862 and reprinted in 1875, has been for some years inaccessible, and because I think it is a book that will interest English fencers.

An interesting and appreciative account of the book is given in the introduction to the volume devoted to fencing in the Badminton Library, together with some criticism of the author. The would-be fencer is cautioned that the Baron de Bazancourt is 'a very expert literary dodger' whose specious arguments must be studied with the greatest caution. The warning note is no doubt wise in a book intended for the English fencer, for English fencing certainly shows no tendency to be excessively correct, but is rather inclined to err in the other direction. But no fencer who reads the work attentively can fail to derive from it a real profit, and, I hope, a real pleasure. The keynote of the book is that a fencer must fence with his 'head.' Bazancourt generally calls it 'instinct,' or 'inspiration.' But call it what you will, there can be no doubt that the continual tax that fencing makes on the resourcefulness of the player gives it its subtle and enduring charm. The unforeseen emergencies that have to be faced, and the varieties of play that are encountered in meeting different opponents, make fencing of all sports the least mechanical and the least monotonous.

We are often told that fencing will never be popular in England, because it is no longer required for practical purposes. But does anyone suppose that we are guided by practical

considerations in choosing our sports? Fencing
is a most exhilarating exercise and one that is
particularly suitable for those of us who live a
town life. A dull day in London may be very
sensibly enlivened by a brisk assault. The
luxury of getting into flannels is increased by
the reflection that for an hour at any rate one
will think of nothing but the foils. For no
exercise is so absorbing as fencing. Whether
you are taking a lesson or are engaged in a
friendly combat your whole attention cannot
fail to be occupied. There is room for nothing
else, and on that account alone fencing must
be commended as a mental relaxation of the
highest value.

Compared with boxing, fencing has the
advantage that it can be continued even into
old age. Now, however willing one may be
to be punched and pommelled, there usually
comes a time when it is inconvenient to appear
in public with a black eye or a bruised cheek.
Few men who take to fencing and master the
preliminary stages can make up their minds to
give it up, until they are obliged to do so for
want of time or opportunity.

The cosmopolitan character of fencing is
another point in its favour. Not only through-
out France and Italy, but wherever French or
Italian is spoken, fencing rooms abound, and

the stranger who visits them is sure to be
received with friendly interest and hospitality.
Fencers are always glad to try conclusions with
a new blade, and a very moderate knowledge
of the art may often serve as a pleasant and
informal introduction in a strange country.

The art of translation is perhaps as slippery
and elusive as the art of fence. *L'escrime vit
de loyales perfidies* says the Baron de Bazancourt.
He might have said the same thing of translation. I have endeavoured to give a faithful
rendering of this book. It has equally been
my object to make my version readable. I am
conscious of many defects, and cannot hope to
have avoided mistakes, but if I have sometimes
been perfidious, I trust that I have never been
disloyal.

I have to thank many friends for assistance
and advice, and I am especially indebted to
Mr F. H. Townsend for the spirited series
of fencing drawings that accompany the text.

C. F. CLAY.

London,
October, 1900.

Introduction

I.

WHY have I written this book? I will tell you. For of all the subjects that might have occurred to me, this I am sure is the last in the world on which I should have ever dreamed of trespassing. Accident, however, is apt to take a hand in the most trivial things of this world as well as in the most important. It is continually responsible for the most unlikely events, and it was in fact by accident that I undertook this work, in which I have collected and jotted down remarks that are entirely my own, concerning an art to which I have devoted myself for more years than I care to remember.

I was staying in the country at an old manor house belonging to one of my friends. The litter of autumn, fallen leaves and withering herbage, was scattered over field and woodland. This is a favourite season with poets, when Nature before her winter sleep affects a serene and melancholy air, that inclines to reverie and lends wings to fancy. The season also favours sportsmen. Coverts in which the game has hitherto found shelter are no longer impenetrable, and every day the wind robs the poor persecuted beasts of some fraction of their shield of verdure. At my friend's house there were no poets, but there was instead a large shooting party. We used to take the field after breakfast, and come home towards dusk, all of us as tired as a man has a right to be when he has done six or eight hours' walking. After dinner we invariably adjourned to the smoking room, and spent the evening in discussing things in general over our cigars.

II.

One evening—I quite forget how it came about—we found ourselves talking about fencing. Some one's casual remark, as erratic as the blue wreaths of smoke that floated vaguely towards the ceiling, was taken up by some one else, and led to other remarks, which gradually became more definite and finally solidified into a conversation.

One can always talk, and one enjoys talking about a subject in which one is interested. That is one of the general truths. And as I have always been devoted to the practice of arms, I found myself talking at some length and expounding some views of my own, which I have tested by practical experience and observation till they have established themselves in my mind as axioms.

I was listened to with attention, though there were few fencers present. And after all the art of fence does furnish a most interesting fund of conversation—the art of skilful fighting at close quarters, which implies a knowledge of theory combined with a trained power of execution, which taxes eye and hand, vigour and judgment, and brings into play every faculty of mind and body, each doing its part, and each in turn supplementing and reinforcing the other.

III.

"Are you aware," said one of my friends, "that these are the secrets of the sword that you are revealing to us?"

"Only," I replied, "those secrets which I happen to know. But really you have hit upon the right word, for the secrets of the sword are innumerable. It is a Proteus in the hand that orders it, and obeys the least motion of the will with the quick docility of an attendant spirit. It can be the insolent and overbearing bully, it can be the wary and diplomatic courtier. At one moment it is all menace, a keen attacking point, the next it changes to a protecting shield.

"But alas for our poor faithful servant; to-day the sword and its secrets are almost forgotten, or at least but little valued. There was a time, and a time not so very remote, when a knowledge of sword-play was considered one of the credentials of a gentleman. Apply that test now; apply it to yourselves. We have here in this room a large number of gentlemen met together, and I do not doubt that each one of you could make good his title to gentle birth, and that in more ways than one ; and yet how many of you would be seriously embarrassed if you were required to manipulate a sword ! How many of you, if you will allow me to say so, would make but a very pitiful exhibition of yourselves ! "

I saw by the smile that went round the room that my remarks were only too well founded.

" Of course," I continued, " I know the usual answer :—'True,' you will say, 'we may be duffers, but we are not afraid of fighting.' Yes, you are not afraid of fighting, that is to say you are willing to be killed by the first bully, who chooses to force a quarrel upon you. Brave words truly ! But after all is it worth while to be the owner of so many talents, youth and strength, a cultured mind, a healthy body, and yet not even to know how to defend your life ?

" I am reminded of the story told of a certain General. When one of his officers, who disagreed with him on the policy of some strategic move-ment, had said :—' Well, General, when the time comes I will show you that I know how to die.'

' Don't be a fool, Sir,' replied the General, 'your duty is not to see that you get killed, but to take care that you don't '."

"Surely," suggested one of my friends, "the real difficulty is that it takes years of conscientious and continual application to make even a moderate fencer."

"Quite a mistake, I assure you."

"Why, only the other day I happened to pick up one or two books about fencing and glanced through them. I assure you, they really are appalling."

"There we have it," I exclaimed, "and with that word you go over bag and baggage to the enemy's camp. You are not the first to be appalled, merely because the professors have omitted to caution the reader, that they cannot in the exercise of their craft afford to be otherwise than omniscient, and that their omniscience must be aired. It is because they are afraid of being taxed with ignorance, or of being rated as less men than their predecessors, that they insist on science at any price; science they must have, interminable and unmitigated science, and so they produce their laborious treatises, monuments of erudition, but as you say—appalling.

"For my part, after reading and rereading, with the most scrupulous attention, everything that has been written on the subject, I remain convinced of this, that if I were writing a manual of fencing my first object would be to get rid of the alarming jargon of technical terms, which are supposed to be indispensable—a formidable array, quite enough, I freely admit, to give pause to the most resolute, and to blanch the cheek of the keenest aspirant."

" Ah, you are quite right," said my host with the air of a man who had made the experiment. "How much the art and the professors too would have gained, if they had only studied simplicity, and taken the trouble to make themselves intelligible."

IV.

The conversation, you see, was getting on.

"Unfortunately," I continued, "most of the professors who have committed themselves to paper have thought otherwise. They plunge into interminable dissertations on the denomination of thrusts. They use words which, it is true, may be found in the dictionary but which have an unfamiliar appearance. For instance they talk about the hand *in pronation* or *in supination*, instead of simply saying the hand with the nails turned up, or the hand with the nails turned down.

"Others have devoted their energy to working out combinations and classifications of feints, parries, and ripostes, distinguishing between them by the nicest shades of difference, and to devising subtleties of terminology, even going so far as to compile and exhibit with the pride of a collector a prodigious catalogue of twelve thousand five hundred strokes[1]. What memory could possibly contain them?

"Now I, on the contrary, should have spared no pains to prove that it is perfectly possible to learn the practical management of the sword without a superhuman effort, and that sword-play is worth cultivating as a delightful exercise and one of the finest kinds of sport.

"For unfortunately we have to remember that Latin, which one uses so seldom, perhaps once or twice after leaving college, and Greek, for which one has even less occasion, are considered useful and even necessary parts of polite education, but that such things as swimming,

[1] Lafaugère, *Traité sur les Armes.*

which may on an emergency be the means of saving your life, or fencing, which is one of the most healthy of athletic exercises, the best thing in the world for developing and bracing a feeble youngster, and which enables you to defend yourself if you are challenged by a bully or assaulted by a blackguard, are reckoned merely frivolous accomplishments. And it is generally recognised of course that it is not right to waste time on mere accomplishments.

"I mentioned Latin and Greek, which we all learnt more or less at school. Well, do you suppose that the man who is going to make learning his profession carries his studies no further than the rest of us, however scholarly some of us may be? No, of course he must go deeper and examine the remotest bearings of the particular branch of knowledge, which he will presently have to teach.

V.

"If you want a still more striking analogy, take horsemanship. Most men learn to ride, and can as a matter of fact manage a hack in the park without making an exhibition of themselves, or even join the road-riders when it is a question of following the hounds. But do you suppose that the mere man on horseback takes the trouble to acquire the whole art of horsemanship, the severe mastery which the professional requires, the 'high airs' of the school rider? Does every one study the fundamental principles, and analyse the nice distinctions, which go to make the finished equestrian,— such a man as the late Mr Astley?

"How few there are who attain or pretend to attain this rare degree of excellence. And yet they alone can tell you how much perseverance, how much continual application, and downright drudgery they have had to go through. For you may be quite sure that perfect mastery of any kind whatever can only be the matured result of extraordinary diligence. Yet you seldom meet a man who cannot ride tolerably, and you find that men ride with more or less grace, or freedom, or vigour, according to their natural disposition, and gradually perfect their style, or if you prefer it, unconsciously complete their education by the growth of habit and experience. It is just the same with fencing.

"If you would be an accomplished swordsman, you will certainly require years of hard work, close application, and incessant practice. But do you need this recondite skill? What would you do with it? You would find it embarrassing. All that you need as men of leisure, is to be able to use a sword as you do a horse, for your amusement, and when you have occasion for it. And observe I say for your amusement, for no sport is so attractive for its own sake, or so engrossing as the practice of arms."

"You are of opinion then," remarked the Comte de C..., "that a man can learn to use a sword without devoting to it more time and trouble than he does to riding?"

"I am sure of it; but don't misunderstand me, I mean riding in the sense of sticking on. In fact, without driving the analogy too hard, I should say that for both exercises a year at the outside is all that is required to obtain useful and solid results. And I should add that after a few months' trial you will find that you cannot resist the fascination that belongs unmistakably to both these sports. Surely that is not too much to ask for putting you into good trim, and teaching you how to protect yourself?"

"Then, why don't they say so?" some one remarked.

"Well, I do say so," I replied. "And what

is more I will make my words good, if one of these days you care to continue this discussion."

I was unanimously called upon to keep my word, and that the next day.

"Well, to-morrow then," I replied, "I shall do my best to convince you ; but you don't give me much law."

"What, with twenty-four hours' notice ? "

"There's something in that—I will sleep upon it—and so—good-night."

That is the true history of the making of this book. The following chapters are the record of our conversations, which I have simply put into shape and revised.

The First Evening

Keep the right foot straight.

I.

THE next day after dinner we all reassembled in the smoking-room.

"Well," said my host, "your audience you see is complete, our cigars are alight, and we are ready to give you our best attention."

"Of course," I replied, "you will understand that I have no intention of inflicting upon you a course of instruction. As far as that goes, the books, especially the two that have appeared most recently, by Professors Gomard and Grisier, have said all that is worth saying, and in my

C.   2

judgment perhaps a great deal more. They give too much good advice, too many excellent rules, too many excellent maxims, too many thrusts, feints, parries, ripostes, counter-ripostes, and so forth.

" I am very far from holding with the received doctrine of the necessity or the importance of a great variety of play. I believe that the effectiveness of a skilful fencer depends on the correctness of his inferences, on the alertness and nicety of his judgment, on quickness of hand and precision of movement, whether in attack, parry, or riposte, rather than on a very varied play, which necessitates a much more elaborate training, and so far from being of any real use serves only to perplex the mind.

" The alphabet of fencing, if you will allow the expression, is as fixed and immutable as any other alphabet. Its characters are ascertained and definite motions, which are combined in accordance with the structure and balance of our organism, the natural action of the muscles, and the flexibility possible to the limbs and body. I do not set up for a schoolmaster, and shall not attempt to teach you this alphabet. I assume that you are already acquainted with it. All that I shall do, or at all events try to do, is to discuss the theoretical principles, for apart from them the material factors are only so much dull and senseless machinery

"I shall try to keep within bounds, and to advance a few simple arguments, to convince you that swordsmanship is neither so slow nor so perplexing as you are inclined to suppose. Above all, I hope you will not allow me to forget that this is a conversation. Remember that you are at liberty to make any remarks that occur to you. That is part of the bargain."

Several of my friends assured me that I need have no anxiety; they did not mean to let me off too easily.

II.

"To begin then; my first object will be to make my meaning perfectly plain. The thing to do will be to take fencing in its broad outlines. It would be labour thrown away to enter the bewildering labyrinth of those interminable details, which after all are nothing more than the mathematical extension of elementary prin-ciples, which may be continued to infinity.

"Fencing in its infancy had to feel its way;

2—2

its methods were yet to be found, its possibilities to be explored. Little by little, as one period succeeded another and the art became in many respects perfected, changes were introduced, and especially changes that tended to greater simplicity. Old theories became old fashioned and were thrown aside to make room for new doctrines.

" Fencing, in fact, was developed like most other things. But we must not lose sight of the fact that the early methods of the old masters, both in Italy and France, date from the sixteenth or seventeenth century, and that the weapons employed in those days differed materially from ours in shape, weight, and function. The change of weapon has naturally led to a change of method.

" It would doubtless be interesting to the antiquary to trace the successive changes that have taken place in sword-play, and to compare it as it exists to-day with what it was in 1536, when Marozzo wrote his treatise on the sword. (Pray excuse my erudition.) The sword of that period was a wide straight blade with two cutting edges. I need not say that Marozzo was Italian. The first French work on the subject was, I believe, a treatise by Henri de Saint-Didier, which was published in 1573, and dedicated to Charles IX. At that time France was a long way behind Italy, where for twenty years already the edge had been abandoned for the point.

"It is not my intention to retrace the abstruse history of the development of swordsmanship; such an inquiry would, however, prove that in all ages the new truths were invariably denied before they established themselves as accomplished facts. There is no need then, as you will doubtless be relieved to hear, to discuss the systems of antiquity; we will pass over the intervening periods without further preface, and come down at once to modern times.

III.

"We are told to draw a hard and fast line between two schools,—probably for the convenience of putting ourselves in the right and our opponents in the wrong.

"For my own part, and speaking seriously, I fail to recognise more than one. True, that one may be regarded from several points of view. I can distinguish three very clearly, but these different aspects are very far from being distinct in the sense of clearly defined natural orders. I will describe three kinds of play, which are adopted by fencers according to fancy.

" The first is fencing regarded as a graceful athletic exercise, contrived very much on the lines of a ceremonious dance, the interlacing movements of the combatants, as they close and fall back to their original positions, recalling the figures of a quadrille. One might almost say that the simplest example of this method is the single combat of melodrama, the stage duel with its concerted movements, and that it finds its most perfect expression, or, if you prefer the phrase, attains its object in the execution of a series of *voltes* and *passes* or dodgy side-steps, a complicated succession of attacks, parries, and ripostes, skilfully delivered, and brought off strictly in accordance with prescribed regulations.

" The second is fencing conceived as an exact science. Here it is 'the noble art' that calls for profound study and arduous research. The student must explore its truths and consider them in all their bearings, pursue theory to its remotest ramifications, and drag to light its most reluctant secrets. . Solid hard work and assiduous application, such as science always demands of her votaries, backed by physical and intellectual resources naturally fitted to the task, are the only means which will enable you to achieve this consummate skill, the highest degree of attainment in the art. You will not be surprised when I say that the annals of the sword record but few names of undisputed preeminence, new stars that mark the epochs in its history.

"The third is fencing considered from the point of view of practical self-defence. In this case the method is fashioned, so to speak, by personal inspiration, and is impressed with the stamp of individual character. This is the real thing, battle in deadly earnest, complete with all the terrors and sudden crises of warfare. Instead of passes ingeniously complicated, and foiled by parries as scientifically elaborate, steel clashes with steel, intent on forcing somewhere a passage for the point. The game becomes a fight, and a fight all the more grim, because the fighting animal is reinforced by science, and chooses from her armoury the weapons that make him strong, rejecting whatever is cumbrous or likely to obscure his 'native hue of resolution.'

"We now see the difference between the two styles,—call them schools if you like. One

wishes to preserve intact and unalloyed the
ancient academical traditions,—I had almost
called them the traditions of the dancing
master, — while the other inclines to what
nowadays we call realism. Is that a gain or
a loss? At the present time everything tends
to realism, but we are not, so far as I know,
obliged to admit that the dream is the type
of perfect beauty, and the real the type of all
that is ugly and bad. We live in a practical
age, perhaps too practical. Sometimes one may
regret that it is so; but what other result could
you expect to follow from the convulsions that
have so frequently shattered it? The ideal,
scared by the noise and confusion of our revolutions, so often repeated, so seldom foreseen,
has used its wings to some purpose, and taken
flight to a world far removed from ours.

IV.

"You will tell me that my comment is too
grave for my text, but you know as well as I do
that small things and great are linked together
by bonds, which may be invisible but are none
the less real."

"Every age," remarked one of my friends, "has its own manners and customs. We no longer live in the days when every gentleman carried a sword at his side and as a matter of course knew how to use it. The taste for fencing is not so universal that we are all impatient to be initiated into its inmost mysteries. Some of us may not have sufficient leisure or sufficient inclination ; we are too busy or too lazy. I believe that what most men think about it can be put in a very few words :— '*We don't want to fight but*—if we must, we should like to be able to show our teeth and fight like gentlemen,' that is all that the average man wants with fencing."

"Quite right," chimed in the Vicomte de G. with a laugh, "we only want just so much of it as will serve our private ends."

"All that you say," I continued, "is true, but it is not the whole truth, as you would readily admit if you paid a visit to one of the fencing rooms of Paris. If you happened, for instance, to drop in on my friend and esteemed master, M. Pons, you would find a gathering of amateurs, who are devoted to the practice of arms, who keep up the traditions with taste and culture, and understand thoroughly well how a sword ought to be used.

"But, to be quite fair, I must hasten to add that the prowess and prestige of these brilliant players would not suffer by the simplification of sword-play. The point I wish to make is that a treatise on fencing for the use of gentlemen, who have so little time to spare and so much to waste, is a book to be written, a book of real utility and importance, and indeed almost indispensable. I have put my finger on a felt want, and if you will allow me I will briefly explain how I think such a book ought to be written, and what it ought to teach. I know, of course, that I shall be violently contradicted, but after all—I know that I am on the right track.

V.

"I have told you that we are asked to make an absolute distinction between two schools of fencing. Obviously it is the new school that is wrong, and, as I happen to belong to that school, you must give me leave to defend it, or, at all events, to explain its tendencies, logically, theoretically, and practically."

"Take care, Sir," a voice was heard to remark, "those three words are decidedly appalling."

"Don't be afraid," I answered, "they are not so formidable as they seem at first sight. You will find that if we thresh out the general principles, what I have to say presently will be much simplified and easier to follow.

"You often hear men say: 'There is no pretty fencing nowadays. It has relapsed into its primitive brutality.'

"Not at all," I should answer, "it has come back to its proper object. For consider,—an exercise, an art which starts with the fundamental idea of a fight between two men who are thirsting for each other's blood, cannot be regarded as a mere amusement, or as an academical study in civility and good manners. One might argue with some effect, that to sacrifice the first essential principle of the art to superior refinements, which were really too exclusive, was a risky game to play, and that, sooner or later, the players were sure to discover that fact to their cost. Now I should maintain that the revolution, which has been brought about, is a clear advance, and only brutal, if you will have it so, because it is the assertion of the brutal truth.

"With the exception of the few who have the ambition to make themselves accomplished swordsmen, men you meet in the fencing room do not as a rule come there to sit at the feet of the professor, and imbibe the mystic lore of scientific theory which he expounds, but rather to be drilled and disciplined in the practical use of the sword which he holds in his hand.

"As a young man I was passionately fond of fencing; I worked at it with enthusiasm; my diligence and devotion were untiring. Among my contemporaries were several very strong amateurs, really skilful swordsmen, experts worthy of the best days and most glorious traditions of the sword. I am thinking of such men as Ambert, Caccia, Choquet, Lord Seymour, the Marquis de l'Angle and others, a group of amateurs well able to hold their own with the most skilful masters. I believe that at that time, and I give you this as my sincere conviction, fencing reached as high a level as at any period in its history.

VI.

"It was the opening of a new era. Hitherto the art had advanced along a narrow track. Now the old ways suddenly broadened out. Old methods were superseded. Fencing was no longer treated as an academical accomplishment, a graceful exercise in courtly skill and bearing, from which originality was barred. It had become something more than the glib repetition of set phrases, that had been got by heart from a book and carefully rehearsed. The new movement, as it may well be called, though it abandoned the perfect manner, which had grown too perfect, brought our elusive art back to regions less celestial, I readily admit, but at the same time brought it face to face with other than imaginary difficulties.

"The art received a new impetus. 'Natural fighters,' men equipped with abundant energy and assurance, who were convinced that all that was necessary for self-defence was a general athletic training such as they possessed, called the fencer's skill in question. Regarded as fencing their style may have been faulty, not to say atrocious, but they confronted the fencer with this logical dilemma :—'You are a master of the sword or an accomplished amateur, I, on the other hand, know nothing about it. Hit me and do not let me hit you. That is all I ask. I shall fight by the light of nature and do what I can ; you will be strictly scientific and keep to your rules.'

"To my mind the only way to silence an opponent of this sort was to take sword in hand, and literally demonstrate to him that he was equally ignorant and incapable. This course, however, did not commend itself to others, who were content to fight this modern hydra, which reappeared every day in some new shape, with— contempt.

"The professors gnashed their teeth and swore, though a few of them kept their temper :—

'Is our Art then,' they declaimed, 'a mere delusion, a fallen idol ? Are we to prostitute and expose it to the barbarous excesses of a brutal and ignorant mob ? Are we to join in an outlandish Babel, where every one claims to be heard in his own tongue, some jargon which no one can understand ? '

"There certainly was something in this line

of argument, however magisterially it might be stated. But at the same time it was impossible to deny that there was, wrapped up in these ungainly eccentricities, a real truth, which could not be entirely neglected. For among the noisy crowd, who would have liked to set their fads upon a pinnacle, one found fencers of experience, men who by long training and the use of scientific method had acquired sound judgment and thorough workmanship. These men, it is true, had the courage to trample on the ancient superstitions, and gladly welcomed the widening of the field, which would give ample room, and scope for every kind of bias.

"It was clearly a revolution, and declared itself by the unmistakable signs of all revolutions, by its aggressive attitude and by its onslaught on old ideas and traditions, which till then had been thought unassailable.

"Molière's famous maxim,—'Hit and don't be hit back,'—asserted itself triumphantly. Truth and falsehood went hand in hand. The thing to be done was to winnow the chaff from the corn, and not reject the whole as worthless.

VII.

"Well, let us now see if we can sum up the real changes which the new school introduced.

"As a matter of fact it proposed absolutely none that was unreasonable. Its tenets amounted to this :—'A fencer must be judged not so much by his graceful attitude and classical style, not so much by his masterly command of precise execution, as by his power of quickly conceiving and quickly delivering the right attack at the right moment.

'When once a beginner has learnt the rudiments of sword-play ; when he has learnt that the movements of hand and body must correspond, and maintain an even balance in every position ; that the wrist must be quick to follow the adverse blade and form a close parry, without flying wild and wide in uncontrolled disorder ; when he can appreciate the value of a step to the rear and the value of a step to the front ; when he has grasped the danger to which he is exposed in making a complicated attack, and realises that the effectiveness of a simple attack depends on the power of seizing the critical moment,—then he should be left to follow his natural instinct, and allowed to exercise his own judgment in making use of the knowledge he has acquired.'

"You should not say to him :—'We must now describe an exact circle, beyond which, by thought, word, or deed, you must not budge. You find it a more natural position, and easier for attack and riposte, to lean your body forward and double yourself up. It cannot be helped, you are required to keep the body upright by the rules of classical fencing.

'You prefer to keep out of distance, because you find that at close quarters your nervous dread of a surprise attack or of a quick thrust is disconcerting and disturbs your equanimity. You must not keep out of distance. You are required to keep the prescribed distance and to join blades.

'You are afraid of attacks on the sword, such as beats, binds, and pressures, or of surprise attacks, and to avoid them you refuse to engage your adversary's blade. You must not refuse. You are required to engage swords by the rules of the game ; only bad fencers attempt to avoid the engagement.

'You attack in the low lines, perhaps you

hit your opponent below the belt. Quite true, the hit would be fatal in a duel, but in sword-play it is considered a foul blow ; the code does not allow it, therefore the hit is bad.'

VIII.

" This sort of thing is mistaken prejudice. The assault ought to be a sham fight.

" It follows that everyone should have liberty of action. Do not attempt to force A. to be graceful and elegant, if he is not built that way. Permit B. to develope his own style in his own fashion, and do not try to make him a servile copy of yourself, merely for the sake of empha-sising your superiority. If he makes mistakes, take advantage of them, that is the most con-vincing kind of correction. If his play is dangerous but incorrect, show him that you can be at once correct and dangerous.

" In short we ask for a fair field and no favour for every sort of style and theory that is based on a study of the weapon. Science you know is the result of intelligent application. Do you seriously believe that these fencers are devoid of science, because they refuse to be judged by your standard, or because they try

to obtain new results, where you persist in seeing
nothing but annoying tricks?

"You must allow one of two things. Either
the methods which these fencers employ, their
plans of attack and defence, are based on policy
and their knowledge of the weapon, and their
source of inspiration is the same as yours; in
that case they are justified by results, they have
teeth and can bite, and are not the easy prey,
which you expected to find them. Or on the
contrary, they go to work without judgment,
they let fly at random, and advance or retire
without any notion of time or distance, their
parries are wide and weak, without any sense of
touch, their attacks uncertain, wild and inco-
herent. In that case they are not dangerous.
Chance may perhaps protect them once, but you
with your experience and skill of course will
easily defeat them, and their slap-dash play will
lead them promptly into every trap which you
choose to set for them.

IX.

"Such is the controversy, the great quarrel
between the two schools, the feud between the

white rose and the red. I have attempted to explain it to you in its general outlines as clearly as I possibly could. You will find it easier to understand the details, which we shall consider when we continue this discussion."

"What will your subject be to-morrow?" asked my host.

" I really cannot say," I replied. "It would be difficult to lay down a regular plan. No doubt something will turn up to talk about. And, by the way, this morning I noticed in the library one or two old books about sword-play, and I shall try to find time to turn them over."

The Second Evening

The legs are springs.

I.

IT began to dawn upon me that my under-
taking was more serious than I had
anticipated, and that I had let myself in for
some uncommonly hard work; for I should
have to advance solid reasons in support of
the theories that I had so rashly propounded.
I had committed myself to nothing less than
the exposition of a system to men who, for
the most part, knew nothing at all about sword-
play, and could not be expected to understand
the meaning of the technical terms. I should

have to be clear and precise and ready to answer any questions that might be put to me.

I was particularly anxious to carry my little audience with me, because I venture to think that no gentleman's education is complete without some knowledge of fencing, and I consider that parents and guardians are much to blame if they fail to recognise the two-fold importance of this indispensable exercise, which not only strengthens and developes the learner's body, but also insures his life.

"Ah," I exclaimed, as I joined the company in the smoking-room, where we met every evening, "my audience I see is before me."

"You have kept your audience waiting," said my host, "and we have kept an armchair waiting for you. Sit down, and begin as soon as you please."

"Thank you," I replied sitting down,—"I will begin at once."

II.

"I remarked, yesterday, that the art of fencing would greatly benefit by simplification, and that it does not require such formidable and protracted study as some of the text-books by their elaborate display of intricate and interminable combinations would lead you to suppose.

" The elementary principles of sword-play are four in number. They are these :—

SIMPLE ATTACKS.   COMPOSITE ATTACKS.
SIMPLE PARRIES.   COMPOSITE PARRIES.

" Here is a table of the attacks and parries :—

SIMPLE ATTACKS.

The Straight Thrust.   The Disengagement.

COMPOSITE ATTACKS.

One, two.   Feint disengage.
Beat straight thrust.   Feint cut over.
Beat disengage.   Cut over and disengage
in tierce or quarte.

SIMPLE PARRIES.

Quarte.   Seconde.
Tierce.   Low Quarte, or Quinte.

COUNTER PARRIES.

Counter-Quarte.   Counter-Tierce.   Circle.

III.

"My classification, you see, is not very complicated."

"But," some one objected, "you are surely forgetting to name an immense number of strokes and parries; for it is impossible that the long lists of names, which are given in the books, and the directions for the various passes, which have the air of cabalistic formulae and are about equally intelligible, can be reduced to such simple terms."

"I am willing to forget them," I replied, "in fact more than willing, for I am convinced that they only serve to distract the learner's mind. The simpler the principles, the simpler the practice. Give him fewer things to do, and he will do them more easily, and he will certainly learn to do them in a shorter time.

"I have always said that a text-book of fencing, which contained nothing that was superfluous, would not fill a volume but might be written out on a sheet of notepaper, and besides, I would have you notice that several

of the attacks, parries, and ripostes included
in my list might logically have been omitted,
because they are simply different ways of
executing the same movement.

" For instance, what I have called " *One, two* "
is the combination of two *disengagements*, one
delivered in quarte, the other in tierce. The *beat
straight thrust* is the combination of a *beat* on
the sword with a *straight thrust*. The *beat
disengage* is simply a *beat* followed by a *disengagement*. *Feint cut-over, feint disengage* are
in like manner the different methods, which are
most commonly used, of executing the *straight
thrust* or the *disengagement*, the two fundamental
strokes of sword-play.

" Even the *cut-over* is really a sort of *disengagement*, since it starts from the same position,
is aimed at the same point, and may be met by
the same parries. The only difference is that
the *disengagement* passes under the blade, while
the *cut-over* passes over the point. The *cut-over
and disengage in quarte* is the same movement as
counter-quarte, conceived and executed in the one
case as an attack, in the other as a parry. *Cut-
over and disengage in tierce* is related in precisely
the same way to *counter-tierce*.

"You see, then, that the multiplication of strokes, far from extending to infinity, may be reduced to very narrow limits. And I am firmly convinced, that if you transgress these limits you are at once involved in endless confusion, which you ought to be very careful to avoid.—You will, I am sure, admit the force of my argument.

"The attacks and parries which I have described traverse all the lines which are open to the passage of the sword, that is to say *the high and low lines, the inside lines and the outside.* The fencer whose mind is set free from the perplexity of parries complete and parries intermediate and so forth, understands more clearly the materials that are available for his combinations, and the measures that he must take to meet the adverse attack.

"The lucidity of his mind is reflected even in the movement of his hand which goes straight to its mark without hesitation or confusion. Speed and freedom of delivery follow as a matter of course. And we must not forget that quickness of hand, combined with what may be called fencing judgment, is of all qualifications the most important, the most necessary, the most vitally indispensable.

IV.

"We may as well follow up the turn our
conversation has taken, and pass under review
without further preface the three watch-words of
swordsmanship :—

JUDGMENT;   CONTROL;   SPEED.

The man who should master these three
would be the pattern of the perfect fencer.

"Well, what of fencing judgment? Why in
the world should you be afraid of it, as though
it were the hundred-headed hydra that guards
the sacred portals? What is it but that part
of the understanding that we all bring to bear
on the conduct of everyday life? Nothing in
human affairs however trivial or however great
can be done without it.

"Fencing judgment implies more especially
distrust, cunning, a wise caution, the power of
interpreting the dumb language of the sword,
the faculty of drawing correct inferences. These
faculties are in the first instance directly stimu-
lated by the master's lessons, and natural
intelligence, acting without any conscious effort

on your part, combined with experience, will make the good seed grow. Do not concern yourself about it. Over-anxiety always has a most disturbing effect on the mind.

"The other night when I spoke of the alphabet of fencing, I had a special object in view. There is a language of the sword, by which questions are asked and answered. As soon as you have learnt the words you can speak and understand it. To admit that it is necessary to make a separate study of every possible phrase implies that a simple and straightforward method of instruction, which I hold to be of the highest importance, is unattainable.

V.

"In like manner the faculty of control is a thing that may be gradually acquired by practice. It is the result of imparting a supple 'temper' to the wrist and body, and consists in the knitting up of the various operations into one continuous movement. But, as in the case of fencing judgment, so here, the desired result

cannot be obtained all at once. It is the first
and most natural consequence of your master's
instructions. It comes of daily practice and you
must patiently watch and wait for it, as you
might wait for a peach slowly ripening on a
sunny wall. Let it grow upon you like a
habit, by slow degrees, till it becomes a second
nature.

"Speed, not of course mere quickness of
hand, but the rapid execution of every movement, is one of the fencer's great resources,
whether in attack, parry, or retreat. It is to
my mind the main point to be insisted on from
the very first.

"And, accordingly, I think that the master
should be careful not to overdo the sort of
teaching, that consists in delivering a running
commentary such as this:—'Steady now: not
too fast: take your time about it: think what
you are doing: keep your hand in order: mark
each motion: at the word *one*,—and so forth:
don't hurry, you will go fast enough by and by.'

"It is certainly useful to practise the hand
by exercising it on the master's jacket, but it is
useless to practise it by slow movements. First
explain how the stroke is to be executed, and then
without more ado make your pupil get into the

way of taking it quickly. Slowness is convenient, because it renders execution easy, but the ease of execution that is derived from it is dangerous, because it reacts on the judgment and accustoms the mind to lazy ways. Your object is, no doubt, to bring the hand under control and analyse the stroke in detail, but if the result of your teaching is that your pupil falls into a sluggish habit, you are sowing the seeds of a vice, which you will probably never succeed in extirpating.

"Suppose you are teaching a child to walk, you are not surprised that his first steps are wavering and unsteady, and that he cannot plant his feeble feet firmly on the ground. You hold him up, but you let him walk. In due time he learns to use his strength, as a bird learns to fly. The young fencer is the child learning to walk. As his knowledge and experience gradually expand, many faults will disappear of themselves, or will be more easily seen and corrected by his maturer judgment.

"Speed is a mechanical force, unreasoning, unconscious, but a force capable of development. You must add fuel to the fire and not allow it to go out. Do you suppose that all you have to do is to change the word of command :— 'Now do quickly what you have done slowly

hitherto'? Your new command introduces a
new idea and creates new difficulties.

"Such, speaking generally, are the essential
principles of fencing. I cannot say whether I
have succeeded in showing you clearly how
simple the lesson on these lines may be made,
or how far I have been able to reassure those,
who have inadvertently opened a treatise on
sword-play and have fought shy of the subject
ever since, but I am convinced that a course of
instruction such as I suggest would produce
very good results.

"To explain myself more fully, as I am
talking among friends and there are no professors present, I will go on to tell you briefly
how I should set about teaching the use of the
sword.

VI.

" I should expect my scholar during the first
month to give up *half an hour a day* to foil
practice, and after that to keep it up *three times
a week*. My first lesson would be devoted to

showing him theoretically and practically the vital importance of establishing a perfect concert or balance between the various movements. This is the fundamental principle of all athletic exercises, and applies equally to riding, swimming, gymnastics, and to fencing:

"I should make him advance and retire, lunge and recover, taking care not to lose his balance. This first lesson is sufficient to enable the least intelligent to understand the mechanism of the different movements, which are based on the natural and instinctive faculties of the human body.

"Come, C——," I said, rising from my chair, "unless I am mistaken, you have never attempted to fence. Will you allow me to make use of you by way of illustration?"

"I shall be delighted," replied C——, "but I shall be very awkward."

"Perhaps you will be for the first five minutes. It is the common lot from which no one can escape. Now place yourself 'On guard'; the words explain themselves:—to be on guard, to protect yourself, that is to say to hold yourself equally ready for attack or defence.

"Bend your legs. Let me use an expression

which is perhaps incorrect but which explains my meaning clearly :—Sit well down.

"Your right arm must be half extended. As a general rule the wrist should be at the height of the breast. You will be able later to modify these elementary studies, by adapting them to suit the position which comes to you most naturally. The important thing is to acquire an uncramped easy style, and to keep the body evenly balanced. In this position the sword can most easily traverse the various openings that are offered to it.

"I advance on you. In order to get back and always keep your distance you have only to carry the left foot to the rear, and let the right foot follow it immediately. To advance on me, simply reverse these movements. Bring the right foot forward and follow it up with the left.

"Bravo! you advance like a professor. See that you keep your legs bent and the body upright, so as to be always ready for advance or retreat. If you cannot avoid stooping, lean forward rather than backward. By carrying the body forward you are no more exposed than you were before ; for the body by its inclined position protects itself, presents a smaller surface, and makes it more difficult for your opponent to fix his point, when he might otherwise hit you ; but if you throw the body back, you lose the power of making a quick attack and a quick riposte. Are you tired ? "

" No."

" Good ! That shows that your position is correct, and that it does not cramp your muscles or paralyse any of your movements. You understand, of course, that by standing sideways you present a smaller target to your adversary.

" So much for defence. Now, for the attack.

VII.

" In order to attack, you lunge, by carrying the right leg smartly forward and straightening the left, so as to give the body its full extension.

" Whatever the attack may be, whether simple or composite, the movements of the hand must be completed and the arm absolutely straight, before the lunge is made, though the different movements must follow each other without the least interval.

" It is equally important to remember that the recovery must be as smart as the attack. The great danger of the attack is that it should be too intemperate. for a too intemperate attack leaves you exposed to danger, without strength or speed to escape."

" But," some one asked, " is it really necessary when you are on guard, to arrange the left arm above the head in a graceful curve, and then swing it down to the leg as you lunge ? "

The graceful curve is not an absolute necessity. Place the arm behind your back if you prefer to do so, for if you bring it to the front you drag forward the left shoulder, and thereby expose a larger target to your opponent's point. The arm, you see, acts the part of a rope-walker's balancing pole. It steadies the movements and balances the weight of the body. Since you have a spare arm you must place it somewhere, and if you consider you will see that it is least in the way where I have placed it. It serves a useful purpose in the general arrangement,— that is the only object of the position. I need not refine the point further.

" In fencing, the movements of the body

and limbs are of great importance. All the mechanical part of sword-play depends on the principles which I have just explained. I have now taken the mechanism to pieces and shown you how it is put together.

VIII.

" One word more. What was the reason for choosing this attitude and these movements?

" They were chosen because they are natural and instinctive. Instinct dictated the rule, which is based on experience, on practical necessity, on correct principle.

" What is the object to be attained?

" First, for defence, to allow the limbs their complete liberty of action, their natural elasticity and easy play; secondly for attack, to give the extension of the body its full force.

" Now try to change the position; straighten your legs; you will at once notice the increased difficulty of executing the different movements, whether of attack, defence, or retreat. You lose your balance, and the lunge either precedes the

action of the hand and the extension of the arm,
or follows those movements too late.

"The legs are springs which support the
body and determine its most rapid movements.
If you are out shooting and want to jump a
ditch, you bend your legs in order to obtain the
necessary spring. Or again, if you jump down
from a height, you bend your legs at the moment
your feet touch the ground ; if you do not, your
whole body is jarred.

"I dwell on this point in order to convince
you of its absolute necessity, and to make you
understand clearly the why and wherefore of the
position. But, I repeat, instinct was the first
teacher, experience came later and has only
confirmed the principle.

"One last caution. When once you have
learnt by practice how to harmonise your movements, and have realised how great a power at
a given moment the faculty of making these
movements with ease and rapidity may be, then,
and not till then, venture to take your personal
inclination into account. And if after carefully
weighing the pros and cons you come to the
conclusion that you can, owing to some personal
peculiarity, improve upon the elementary rules
of the lesson, do not hesitate to depart from

them without scruple, but never without good
reason. The best position is that which allows
you complete freedom and perfect balance. But
never forget that all exaggeration is bad, and
that nothing can be worse than the exaggeration
of an ungraceful and ungainly style. That is all
I have to say this evening."

Keep the left shoulder back.

The Third Evening

I.

"WE will continue the course of instruction
of which you have studied at present
only the first page; I am going into very
minute detail, as you see.

"Our scholar now knows the different positions, and can appreciate why they are to be
commended, and what is to be gained by
adopting them. At the next lesson,—and each
lesson would consist of not more than three
bouts of eight or ten minutes each,—I should
show him and make him execute the simple

attacks and the simple parries:—*Disengagements in tierce and quarte, straight thrusts, the cut over, and parries of quarte and tierce.* The attacks will exercise him in the lunge, the parries will improve the flexibility of his wrist.

"I should make him continually retire and advance. I should, even at this early stage, take pains to secure a certain degree of life and speed in his execution, and I should be careful to vary the exercises, and never appeal to his intelligence at the risk of checking the activity of his movements. Sluggishness, I repeat, is a deadly foe, against which every avenue must be closed from the very first.

"Next I should go on to composite parries and composite attacks. I have already named them, and you remember that they are not very numerous. *Counters, double counters,* and combinations of the *cut over* and *disengagement* are the most useful things to practise, because they work the wrist in every direction, and make it both quick and supple.

"Although a great many instructors would say that I am wrong, I should make it my principal aim to form and cultivate a habit of executing all movements at speed. I should insist less on precision of control than on smartness of execution, and at the same time I should call my pupil's attention to the mistakes which he must be most careful to avoid, and to the points of danger where he must exercise the greatest caution.

"I should practise him in retiring quickly, and should make him deliver simple attacks on the march, keeping his blade in position. After a few lessons I should repeatedly place my button on his jacket, if he did not parry quickly enough, or if he was slow on the recovery. In a word I should put plenty of life and go into my lessons from the first, and not allow them to become tedious.

"After every lesson I should direct his serious attention to the principal faults I had noticed, and I should make him understand the dangers to which these faults must inevitably expose him. For instance, if he caught the fatal trick of dropping or drawing back his hand, I should take care to make him attack and riposte in the high lines, in order to get him to carry his wrist high, and vice versa. In this way I should exercise his judgment by making him think, and his hand and body by keeping him closely to his work.

II.

" Above all, the master's lesson must not lose itself in a maze of attacks and parries and ripostes, which in some treatises are as numerous and interminable as the stars of heaven. The strict limitation of the number of strokes to be taught renders their execution proportionately easier, and makes a clear impression on the mind. Experience and fencing instinct teach, far better than any lesson, certain niceties, which give life and finish and character to the play. There you have the lesson complete.

" As the scholar gradually grows stronger, he learns to hold himself correctly, and acquires ease. He understands what to do without being told, and his hand is in a fair way to become the faithful echo of his thought.

III.

" We here touch on another point, where I find myself at variance with nearly all the professional instructors.

"I have read in the books which deal with this subject of 'the danger of premature loose play.' 'You run the risk,' say some, 'of spoiling a promising pupil, and of arresting his future progress, just when he is beginning to form good habits.' Others go further and declare that: 'The instructor who allows his pupil to commence loose play too soon sacrifices by an act of fatal indulgence the whole future of fencing.'

"I do not agree with this view. I cannot even see that it logically applies to those who mean to devote all their time to the study of sword-play, and who are prepared to make a determined effort to reach the topmost summit of this difficult art. Much less, then, to my mind, is it applicable to the generality of men, who have no ambition to become such learned fencers, as we were saying the other evening. The professors wilfully refuse to see this.

"And yet of all arts, the art of fencing may be considered from the most widely different standpoints, and particularly may be approached with very varied degrees of knowledge and application. Is it so very certain that 'premature loose play,' as the professors love to call it, is so pernicious as they think,—the bad seed that cannot fail to produce an evil crop of vices?

Right or wrong, I can only say once more that I am of quite the contrary opinion.

"I fail to see that it is dangerous for a pupil to attempt the assault, when he has learnt by taking lessons for a month,—more or less, according to the progress made and his natural capacity,—to understand the various strokes I have described, and can already execute them with some degree of liveliness and control.

IV.

"Of course I am quite ready to admit that his first assaults, like all first attempts that require a trained habit of mind, cannot be free from mistakes, exaggerations, faults of all sorts. But is not the master there to correct these errors with his lesson, and to bring his pupil, who is inclined to go astray, back to the right path? Cannot the leading strings be read-justed?

"The very fact that the master has had an opportunity of observing the mistakes, to which his pupil is most liable, when left to himself, enables him to devote all his care to overcome and correct them by both practice and precept. More important still, he has also had an opportunity of observing his pupil's bias ; he notices the strokes which come naturally to his hand, the parries he most affects, the natural promptings of his impulse, impetuous or cautious as the case may be.   He makes a study of his artless scholar, who is clumsily feeling his feet, reads him like a book, catches him in the act so to speak, and detects the working of his character, and thenceforward he knows the way in which his studies may be most profitably directed to give full play to his individual temperament.

"The assault teaches the novice what no amount of lunging at the master's pad can drill into him.   It enters him to the sudden emergencies, which in one shape or another arise at every moment, to the movement and exertion and keen emulation of real fighting.   The assault is in fact a lesson subsidiary to the formal lesson, and you may rest assured that the instruction it conveys is equally salutary."

V.

"Then," smilingly remarked the Comte de R., "you are for open war with the existing routine?"

"And with the old traditions. Yes, I am afraid I am. But what can I do? You admit the force of my arguments?"

"Certainly."

"And that fencing taught on my plan loses its terrors?"

"Yes, I quite admit that."

"And in fact it is not really formidable. My system is able to satisfy the requirements of all, and I do not overshoot the mark, by over-anxiety to reach it.

"It is most important to bear in mind that it is not necessary or even desirable to attend all the professor's lectures, to pass all the examinations and finally to qualify as Bachelor of Arms, in order to become a fair ordinary fencer. After all in every art one usually admits the professor's right to dictate the elementary principles of his subject, but after the elementary stage is passed we are not, I believe, always ready to accept the professor's estimate of the importance of the art which he happens to teach. The remark applies equally to music, to painting, to literature, and why not to fencing? Poets we know are nothing if not first-rate, but why should fencers be singled out for this invidious distinction?

"You may judge how firmly my own belief is rooted, when I say that I am as strongly convinced of the good results that follow from 'premature assaults,' as I am of the necessity of making the lesson as simple and as clear as possible.

VI.

"I remember a story told by my friend, M. Desbarolles, an artist who is endowed more liberally than most of my acquaintance with the warm artistic temperament. It is to be found in one of his neatly written essays. He had, it seems, studied fencing for two years under a French master, in Germany I think, when he paid a visit to M. Charlemagne, one of the most famous instructors of the day, to whom he had an introduction.

"He fenced before the professor, and when the bout was over expected to be complimented, under the impression that he had done rather well.

'Will you allow me, Sir, to give you a word of advice?' asked the great man.

'By all means,' replied my friend.

'Then, let me recommend you to give up loose play altogether for at least a year, and confine your attention entirely to the lesson.'

"Good heavens, what amazing perversity, what pompous humbug! M. Desbarolles remarks that he was utterly taken aback, and I can well believe him, but he goes on to say that he accepted the master's verdict, and never had reason to repent it.

"If he had not given his word for the fact, I should certainly have ventured to hope, most sincerely, that his sense of humour was sufficient to save him from following such a piece of advice to the letter, and in any case I am sure that it was quite unnecessary for him to do so, in order to become the charming fencer that he is and one for whom I have the warmest admiration.

"Do not tell me that the quickness of hand and rapidity of movement, the alertness of body and mind required in loose play, can be imparted by the lessons of a skilful instructor, if only he is careful to graduate his instruction in proportion to his pupil's progress. The result is mere clock-work with the professor for mainspring, counterfeit vitality set in motion by the word of command ; a most mechanical use of the intelligence. The pupil cannot go wrong because he is tied to his master's apron-strings. The master's sword shows him exactly where to go with the precision of a finger-post. He is like a man swimming in a cork jacket, practising the motions of swimming at his leisure, and not caring in the least whether these motions would really support him on the surface or let him sink to the bottom.

"That the formal lesson is useful I do not doubt, that it has a monopoly of usefulness I emphatically deny. Why allow it to meddle with and domineer over things which do not concern it? Let it keep its place and refrain from trespassing outside its own dominions.

"The lesson can explain the logic and theory of fencing, it can assign reasons and exhibit the mechanical process, but it cannot deal with the great Unknown, the tricksy spirit, which suddenly starts out on the fencer under every shape and form, always assuming some new disguise and

upsetting in a moment the most perfect theories
and the most scientific combinations.

"The young fencer who undertakes his first
assault is like the heroic youth of the fairy tales,
who leaves his humble cottage and goes out into
the wide world to seek his fortune. Like him
he will meet with many strange adventures,
which will try his mettle, put his character to
the touch, and call into play all the resources of
his intelligence.

VII.

"Perhaps you think that by continually
presenting this question to you in a new light
I am detaining you too long on one part of my
subject. My intention is to bring home to your
minds the conviction I so strongly feel myself.
If you only knew how many striking examples
I have witnessed of the truth of my assertion!

"You may see one of these pupils taking his
lesson. He is a magnificent spectacle; his hand
perfectly correct, a grand lunge, his action
smooth and free; he follows his master's blade
through a cunning series of feints and false
attacks, ripostes and counter-ripostes, his parry

is never beaten ; not a fault, not a single
mistake ; he is an animated illustration of his
master's treatise, which the author with pardon-
able pride displays before you.

"Now in the assault pupils of this type are
far from maintaining their superiority. Their
mechanical agility is paralysed, when it is no
longer set in motion by the accustomed spring.
They know too little and at the same time they
know too much. They find out that the assault
is not the same thing as the lesson. Their
opponent's blade does not accommodate itself
to theirs with the precision to which they are
accustomed ; the touch of the steel no longer
conveys those delicate hints, to which they
formerly responded with such alacrity, and of
course they lose their bearings. They have not
acquired the sort of defence which is ready for
anything, alike for well directed thrusts and
for more eccentric methods of attack, and they
look in vain for a succession of passes strictly
correlated in a systematic order.

"Instead of marching with a swing along the
broad highway to which they are accustomed,
they find themselves lost in a wild and difficult
country without a guide and without confidence.
Habit will perhaps enable them to maintain

some smartness of appearance, but they make few hits, and in spite of their science and the skill, which they undoubtedly possess up to a certain point, they are continually beaten by fencers, who are less scholarly perhaps, but who have been better entered than they to the actual combat, the manifold emergencies of practical fighting, and who have learnt that strange language, by which the sword contrives to reveal the most delicate shades of meaning.

" I have seen this happen so often, that I have taken some trouble to study the question, and I am convinced that if these same pupils had been at less pains to make themselves pedantically perfect in the peaceful and philosophic practice of the lesson, and had been made familiar at an early stage with the changing incidents of the assault, they would have been equally well disciplined, and at the same time really dangerous fencers. Of course I freely admit that exceptions may sometimes be found, but they are the exceptions which prove the rule.

VIII.

"We have now reached a point from which we may survey the thrilling spectacle of the assault, as fencers call the mimic combat, in which desperate and brutal fighting is controlled by skill, the hazardous duel, full of fire and fury, between two combatants, who summon to their aid all that they know or all that they think they know.

"I can say with literal truth, that I have never taken a foil in my hand for a serious assault without feeling a real tremor, and most fencers have experienced and indeed are generally conscious of the same sensation.

"You have listened so kindly to my rough attempt to put together an extemporary course of instruction, that I can confidently claim your attention now ; for we are about to find in this great arena the rival systems face to face. I shall put before you and examine at no great length the various situations which are likely to occur.

"Our imaginary pupil has now become a fencer. He will no longer lunge merely at the master's pad, henceforward he will cover his manly face with a mask. Shall we follow him in his career?"

"We will"; replied my host in tragic tones. "The standard of revolt is raised. Lead on, and we will follow you."

"'Tis well," I answered in the same spirit. "The tryst is here, at the same hour,—to-morrow."

A Parry of Prime.

The Fourth Evening

Coup Double.

I.

THE next day I continued my discourse thus :—

"In the assault with its incessant alarms and perilous crises, in encountering the wiles and avoiding the snares of the enemy, those who use the sword find their 'crowded hour of glorious life,' the hour crowded with illusions and disenchantments, the rubs of fortune, the ups and downs of victory or defeat.

"What legions of cunning counsels and crafty wiles, from the deep-laid stratagem down to the sudden surprise, one finds marshalled in the text-books, and how unmanageable and superfluous they generally are. All that the Spartan mother said to her son when he was setting out for the wars was :—'Be bold, be resolute, be cautious.' Do not her words contain the whole? For all fighting, whether at long range or at close quarters, is very much alike, from schoolboys' games to the most elaborate military operations ; and all the advice of the world may be summed up in the eternal law of attack and defence, which is stated in these four words :—cunning, caution, energy, audacity.

"Deceive your enemy: seize the critical moment to attack him, that is the secret of fighting. Cultivate the mistrust which suspects the hidden snare, the caution which frustrates his plots, combined with the energy and audacity which surmount difficulties ; try to encourage in your enemy a spirit of wanton confidence ; turn a strong position which you cannot carry by a direct attack ; threaten one point when you mean to concentrate your whole strength on another ; draw your adversary by a show of weakness to attack you in your strongest position ; keep your plans secret ; mask your

approaches; and then by the sudden impetuosity
of your attack take him unawares, and if you
cannot secure a victory, contrive a safe retreat.
Such from the earliest times have been the
methods of the greatest commanders.

"The tactics of the field of battle and the
tactics of hand-to-hand fighting are identical,
for the simple reason that skill, or strategy, or
science, call it what you will, are but different
names to express the same idea. These are the
sage counsels; the rest belongs to inspiration,
the inward monitor which in moments of danger
warns us with tenfold insistence, and guides us
right.

"Too much stress is laid on education, too
little on individual intelligence. The lessons
are supposed to have trained and directed this
intelligence. But if your pupil is so wanting in
intelligence that he cannot enter into the spirit
of the game, if he can never rise to the occasion,
and never strike out a line of his own, what can
you expect? You may advise for ever, but his
mind will not respond, he will only listen and
forget.

"It is here that the two schools begin to part
company. I have already given you a general
view of the points in which they differ, and we

need not now recur to the consideration of general principles, with which you are already acquainted.

II.

" If we could return to the past, and witness an exhibition of sword-play as it was understood by the professors of only fifty years ago, what a contrast we should find with the style of our own day, even with our most severely classical style. Our methods would certainly be called revolutionary.

" It was usual not so very long since to display upon the bosom a fair red heart, stitched to the fencing jacket, to show plainly for all eyes to see the spot where hits should be placed. Attacks, parries and ripostes were restricted by convention to a very narrow circle. Any hit that went wide of the mark was accounted execrable and received with the most profound contempt. Modern fencing is inclined to be somewhat less fastidious. Hits in the low line are generally acknowledged. But a hit below the belt! 'You really do not expect me to follow your point down there!' is still the attitude of most fencers.

'Call it a hit if you like, but really it is not fencing. A school of arms, you know, is not a school of surgery, you might leave those base regions to the medical students.'

"You smile, but I assure you that they mean it seriously, without the least sarcasm. It is quite true that any wound in that despised region would be mortal almost to a certainty. That is a detail; and they forget that a sword, though it may be a civil and gentlemanly implement, is still a lethal weapon. It really is very strange to admit that it is wrong to disregard the deadly character of the point when aimed in one direction, but to claim that it is right to disregard it when aimed in another. Yet most men cling to this error with the utmost pertinacity.

"That you should despise a hit in the leg or fore-arm I can well understand. By all means concentrate your whole attention on the protection of the parts of the body which contain the vital organs. But not to use your utmost care, your surest parries, your most anxious precautions to defend the trunk,—high lines and low,—always has been and is still a delusion, a delusion which those who attempt to draw an impossible distinction between the assaults of foil-play and real fighting with sharp swords, vainly ask us to accept as an unassailable article of faith.

"There is a real distinction, for after all foil-play can only be an imperfect representation of real fighting. Our object should be to make the resemblance as perfect as possible, and so minimise the chances on which the ignorant and brutal too confidently rely.

"Let them see that you both know the correct answer to a correct combination, and that you are equally prepared to deal with the wild and disorderly antics of an untutored point.

III.

"You may often hear men say:—'I do that in the fencing room, I should be very sorry to attempt it in a serious fight.'

"Then why attempt it at all? If your judgment tells you that the stroke is good, it is good for all occasions. If it is bad it cannot be justified in any case.

"Always bear in mind that you must pay attention to all thrusts which might prove fatal in a serious encounter, and then if some day you have the misfortune to find a real sword in your hand, you will have the satisfaction of knowing that you are fore-armed by habit against known and familiar dangers. I cannot emphasise this point too strongly.

"In short, the refusal to acknowledge hits however low is a dangerous and a gratuitous mistake. Why should a thrust aimed in that direction not be of its kind as brilliant and meritorious as another? Why should it be boy-cotted? Is there any reason for this mysterious taboo?"

"The old master who used to teach us fencing at school," remarked my host, "would fall foul of you with a vengeance, if he heard you talk like that."

"I do not mean for a moment," I replied, "that I have any preference for hits in the low line, but rather that I am more afraid of them, because I have fenced too often with fencers good and bad not to know how necessary it is to be on one's guard against the dangers of wild play.

"For instance, those who make a practice of

6—2

straightening their arm as they retire nearly always drop their hand, and the point of their weapon, whether they wish it or no, is necessarily directed towards the low line. It is equally inevitable that the same part should be threatened by those who rightly or wrongly reverse the lunge by throwing the left foot back on your attack, at the same time stooping forwards, so as to let your point pass over their head ; and ignorant fencers nearly always hit you there, quite innocently and unintentionally.

"You should therefore guard that part of the body as strictly as you guard the chest, and, by a parity of reasoning, when you meet an adversary who neglects to protect the low line annoy him in that region frequently.

IV.

" It often happens that things that are most neglected in one age become the ruling fashions of the next, just as things once highly honoured may often fall into complete discredit.

"Take this instance. In an old and dusty folio, entitled '*Académie de l'Espée*[1],' which I

---

[1] *Académie de l'Espée*, by Gerard Thibault, Antwerp, 1628.

discovered yesterday banished to the darkest
corner of the library, I found several pages
entirely devoted to the art '*of delivering a stroke
with the point at the right eye.*' The point is
specified because in those days cuts and thrusts
were held in equal favour.

"What do you say to a thrust in the eye?
And yet if you will consult my folio you will
find a collection of plates illustrating all the
passes by which this brilliant stroke may be
brought off.

"You know what is thought now-a-days of
a hit in the face, that is to say on the mask ; we
are taught,—again quite wrongly,—not to take
the smallest notice of it.   And this leads me to
hope that some day we may yet see a revolution,
by which the vulgar belly will claim its rights
and in its turn drive out the lordly bosom.   It
will be rated too highly then, as it is too much
degraded now.   But when did revolutions ever
know where to stop?

"For the assault the one thing needful is
self-reliance.   Trust to your own resources, and
do not imagine that you have to repeat word
for word the lesson that you have got by heart
from your book, but rather look for inspiration
to the resources of your native wit.

V.

"If any one came to me for advice, the course I should recommend, not as a hard and fast rule, but in a general way, would be something of this sort:—Act as much as possible on the defensive, keep out of distance, in order to prevent your opponent from attacking you without shifting his position, and in order to compel him to advance on your point, the most dangerous thing he can do, and without a doubt the most difficult art to acquire. If you make up your mind to stand your ground whatever happens, and to attack always in exact measure, instead of retiring and advancing with quick and irregular movements, and instead of trying to surprise and overwhelm your adversary with combinations for which he is unprepared, you are to my mind simply acting without the least judgment, or rather you are making a perverse blunder.

"Then I should go on to say, always supposing that I was asked for my opinion:—Make a practice of stepping back as you form the parry, if only half a pace. There is everything to be gained by it, and there is no objection to it that I can see, unless it be the strong objection that your opponent will feel to being considerably embarrassed on every possible occasion.

"The advantages, on the other hand, are manifold. By stepping back you increase the effectiveness of the parry, because by withdrawing the body you, in a sense, double the rapidity of the hand. If the attack has been delivered with sufficient rapidity to beat the parry, by retiring you parry twice, the first time with your blade, with which you try to find your adversary's weapon, the second time by removing the body to a greater distance, with the result that the point, which would have hit you if you had stood your ground, does not reach your chest.

"By employing this manœuvre against simple attacks you counteract rapidity of execution, and by employing it against composite attacks or against feints you encounter the last movement forcibly. It is also of service in screening one from attacks made by drawing back the arm, for it often happens if you stand your ground, that your hand starts too soon, and your sword encounters nothing but empty air. It has the further advantage of increasing the fencer's confidence in himself.

"Do not imagine that it hinders the riposte.

It renders it easier and more certain. Nearly always, when a fencer has lunged right out, and —as often happens—does not recover immediately, the two opponents are so close together that it is very difficult to get in the riposte without shortening the arm, and so giving an opportunity for a *remise*.

"The parry and riposte without breaking ground are certainly of value, I do not dispute that, but against the fencers of all sorts, whom you have to meet, and who offer all sorts and kinds of difficulty, they should not be employed except occasionally, and only when they are almost certain to succeed. To my mind it would be dangerous and unreasonable to adopt them as the systematic basis of your play.

VI.

"My reason for insisting so strongly on this point is that I have nearly always found that it is thought to be very magnificent to stand up to the parry, whereas breaking ground is regarded as the shift of a man hard pressed, a last resort when the hand has proved too slow, or when it is necessary to retrieve an error of judgment.

"Now my plan provides you with a second

line of defence, without infringing any of the recognised canons ; it is consistent with the most classical style, and with perfect control of your weapon. And one may well ask why, when two chances of safety are at your disposal, you should deliberately resolve to avail yourself of only one of them ?

"I should accordingly reverse the usual advice, thus:—

'As a general rule and on principle break ground as you parry, either by a few inches or by a clear pace, according to the momentum of your opponent's attack, for by breaking ground I do not mean to say that you are to avoid a hit by continual and precipitate bolting.

'Sometimes stand firm, but only when you are sure that you have at last induced your opponent to develope an attack, which you have long been waiting for him to make.'

VII.

"Unless I know my man, or have come to an understanding with him beforehand, I have very little faith in a prolonged concatenation of parries, ripostes and counter-ripostes, and here again I should try to relieve the mind, as much as may be, from an unnecessary burden, by getting rid of complications instead of multiplying them.

"I look at it in this way. If a fencer has to concern himself with the different lines in which he may be attacked, he must be in a state of continual suspense. He will be continually asking himself whether the attack is coming in the inside line or the outside, in the high line or the low. Thus, in order to parry to advantage and correctly he must wait until his enemy's object is clearly disclosed. Take the case of a simple attack promptly executed ; it is obvious that the attacker must gain a considerable start. True, there are a few fencers, but very few, gifted with so fine a sense of touch, that they can divine their adversary's intention, and read his inmost thought.

"Less gifted mortals should be content with a parry which mechanically traverses all the lines. Such a parry must of necessity encounter the adverse blade forcibly in whichever line the enemy has selected for his attack. When once you have acquired this universal parry the strain is lessened, your mind is more at ease, you are more sure of yourself and feel that you can act with certainty and decision.

VIII.

"There are two kinds of parry, among those which I enumerated the other day, which answer this purpose equally well. The first consists in combining the parry of *tierce* or *counter tierce* with a *cut over* and beat in *quarte*; the second in parrying *counter tierce* and *counter quarte* in succession, and vice versa, or *counter quarte* and *circle*.

"These covering parries though they are technically composite, in practice are fairly simple, and rapidly pass through all the lines that are open to attack. Choose the one which you prefer instinctively, which is another way of saying the one that comes most naturally to your hand. Or, if you like, use sometimes one, sometimes the other."

"But what if this parry is deceived?" asked the Comte de R.

"Well," I answered, "'Deception no cheating' is the fencer's motto. There is no such thing as an attack that cannot be parried, or a parry that cannot be deceived. Sooner or later the fatal moment comes, and superior activity or superior cunning prevails.

"If any professor can invent an attack which it is impossible to resist, or a parry which it is impossible to deceive, I should advise him to take very good care to secure the patent rights of his invention without a moment's delay. He would certainly have no difficulty in floating a company to put it on the market in all the capitals of Europe.

"I have already expressed my opinion that a fencer's strength lies much more in presence of mind and in quickness of hand than in a very varied play. This is so true that the majority of fencers, amateur and professional alike, affect certain favourite strokes; they have favourite attacks, favourite parries and ripostes, and always come back to them as to old friends on whose services they can confidently rely. In the course of an assault the same stroke is often repeated in many different ways; the shape it takes changes with the changing incidents of the fight, and accordingly as it is adapted to suit the peculiarities of the individual against whom it is employed. That is the great beauty of a stroke in fencing.

"Some of you, I know, are not fencers, but there are one or two connoisseurs present, who have studied the art, and are experts. It is to them that I now appeal. As an illustration of my argument I will take the most simple parry, the parry of quarte, and I will ask them if it is not the fact that it constantly changes and undergoes surprising transformations? Sometimes it is a light touch, sometimes a vigorous, almost a violent blow; it may form a high parry, it may form a low parry, it serves for every purpose and answers every call that can be made upon it. Watch the blade as the parry is formed;—perhaps it just meets the adverse blade and suddenly quits it or it may hold and dominate it.

"It is this power of varying the stroke and transforming it at will that marks the true fencer.

"The man, I repeat, who is content to recite his lesson by rote, however well he has learnt it, can never be anything more than a school-boy; call him that or an accomplished parrot, whichever he prefers.

IX.

" I was reading one of the ancient treatises, which arc reposing peacefully on your dusty shelves, my dear C., when I came across the following passage, which rather struck my fancy :—

The law of defence declares that your motions should be the natural motions of a man's body. But, however sacred the dignity of law may be, nevertheless you ought to consider that necessity knows no law, and that it overrides even the weightiest laws of human contrivance.

" That was written in 1600. The maxim is a trifle too sweeping for general application, but it seems to me to be a good and serviceable maxim when applied to sword-play.

" My remarks are perhaps somewhat disconnected. I am simply giving you my ideas at random, as they occur to me. But my main object is to direct your attention to the points which appear to me of some importance.

" After the parries come the ripostes. On this subject a few words will suffice. Never forget that the parry and riposte are twin sisters, whose lives are so closely bound up in each other, that they cannot exist apart. Riposte and parry ought to be so closely allied that the riposte may seem to be the second part of the parry. Therefore, as a general principle, riposte direct, in the line in which you have found the blade. Changing the line wastes time, and gives your adversary an opportunity to pull himself together and make a *remise* or renew the attack. Never, on any consideration, allow yourself to draw back your arm, for then your riposte is lost,—as well throw your purse in the gutter.

"If your judgment tells you that your adversary is waiting for your direct riposte, and has attacked you with the object of drawing it, or if you have noticed that he covers himself effectively on that side, while he leaves you a clear opening elsewhere, then avoid the trap by a disengagement or a cut-over; but only make one feint, never more than one. For, if you do, though you may succeed once, you will probably find out later that your success was dearly bought. It is always wise, you know, to count the cost, and economise your resources, unless you wish to take the straight road to ruin.

X.

"Our chat to-night," I remarked after a moment's silence, "if it has not been very long, has at least been very serious. I only complain that you have not sufficiently interrupted me."

"We have been listening to you," said the Comte de R., "very attentively, because you warned us of the importance of your subject."

"Very well, my dear R.," I replied. "Now just imagine you are in court, and let us hear how you would sum up the case for the benefit of the jury."

"I fancy I can do that rather well," answered R. "Let me try:—The lesson, you say, is the school-room, the assault is the fencer's career, a free field for enterprise, where he must stand or fall by dint of his own unaided genius. The only counsels, which are worth anything, are those which have governed attack and defence from time immemorial. For attack, the union of desperate energy with cool and calculating caution; for defence, firmness, wariness, self-reliance.

"Then, passing from the general question to

points of detail, or execution, I should add :—
It is a great mistake, a piece of inconceivable
folly, to have boycotted, to use your own
expression, hits in the very low lines, because
the fencer is prevented thereby from acquiring
the habit of strictly guarding those parts of the
body, where in a serious encounter any wound
would probably prove fatal.

" As a general rule step back as you form the
parry, to make assurance doubly sure, and to
give greater freedom to your riposte. Stand
your ground only when you think you have
judged the stroke to a nicety, and when you
hold your adversary in a tight place, from which
he cannot escape."

" I am infinitely obliged to you, my dear R.,"
I remarked. " You have summarised most excel-
lently the points that I have worked out in
detail, and you have exactly caught my
meaning."

" Very good of you to say so," answered R.,
" but let me finish :—In order to keep your
wits about you, and to avoid trying to think
of too many things at once, adopt as a rule a
universal parry, which will cut all the lines, and
must meet and drive away your opponent's blade.

Always riposte direct, and be careful on your
riposte to avoid making feints which expose you
to a *remise* or to a renewal of the attack. Does
that satisfy you?"

"You have taken us over the ground most
admirably, my dear Professor. To-morrow, I
propose to discuss the attack, and in this connection we shall have to consider what is usually
called '*le sentiment du fer*,' the fencer's sense of
touch.

"To this sovereign principle we are asked to
swear allegiance, as though it occupied the throne
by divine right. I shall ask you to consider the
pretensions of another claimant of very noble
lineage to a share of the royal honours."

A riposte in tierce.

The Fifth Evening

I.

ALTHOUGH our conversation was quite informal and simply an after-dinner amusement, I found that it involved diligent preparation, especially when I was approaching one of the questions where I was in open conflict with current theories, which are often taken for granted on no better ground than their respectable antiquity.

One of these theories, which is described in fencing language as the importance of judging the blade by touch, I was now prepared to challenge, and I was ready to maintain the superiority of another principle, against which the professors raise their voices, almost with one accord, in a chorus of unmerited abuse. Accordingly when we assembled in the smoking-room, I took my usual seat and began without preface.

II.

"Perhaps I had better explain what is meant by refusing to join blades. It means that, as soon as you have come on guard, you break away from the engagement, and avoid crossing swords with your adversary, instead of allowing the blades to remain in contact.

"This, I consider, was one of the most successful innovations of what it is the fashion to call 'The New School'; and I am therefore very far from sharing the opinions of the professors, who discover in the practice the corruption of the best traditions of sword-play, and declare that the refusal to join blades is equivalent to fencing blindfold, and without judgment; it leads, they say, to mutual hits, and deprives the fencer of one of the finest accomplishments he can acquire, the power of judging the sword by touch.

III.

" Undoubtedly the fencer's touch is a great resource ; I am even willing to allow that it is invaluable, and it is a thing that can only be obtained by practice and perseverance ; it gives lightness and dexterity to the hand, and enables the foil to be manipulated with accuracy and speed.

" It is the refined result that is derived from extreme ease in regulating the extension of the arm, from exquisite subtlety in the use of the fingers, and from precision of play, which involves its victim almost unawares, dismays, and utterly confounds him. I profess the greatest admiration for this consummate power of fence, so seldom seen to perfection. No one can think more highly of it than I do, and on that account I am strongly convinced of the necessity of devising a means to resist it, when it is used against me. I shall perhaps be told to combat it by an equally fine sense of touch ;—but it is still more rare to see a bout of fencing in which the two men are evenly matched in this respect, and general principles should be based on general grounds, not on exceptional cases.

"The man who possesses this consummate sleight of touch may almost be said to control his opponent's blade by the exercise of his will. By a sort of hypnotic influence or fascination he does with it what he pleases. If you refuse the engagement, you create a difficulty for him ; if you do not allow him to bring his blade into contact with yours, you put an impediment in his way, which his skill will doubtless overcome, but with less certainty ; his course is not so clear, and he is no longer completely master of the situation. For if you join blades you are always within striking distance of his point, that is to say he can attack you at any moment without shifting his ground. Now such attacks are exceedingly difficult to stop, even for the most practised hand, especially simple attacks such as straight thrusts or simple disengagements.

"The mind perpetually held in suspense is harassed and distressed, you have no leisure to think for yourself and are demoralised by the slow torture of a constant strain. For, I repeat, it is very rare to find two fencers so evenly matched in this respect that the risk is equally divided.

"In that case I should say :—' Do what you

please.' In the other case :— By refusing the engagement you can at first keep your opponent out of distance, which will compel him to advance in order to attack you, and so give you fair warning of his intention. You are no longer exposed to the paralysing influence of a constantly threatened attack, which destroys your liberty of action and judgment ; you disconcert your adversary by leaving him in the dark as to the line in which he will encounter your blade ; and you can choose your own time, when you are ready to attack or parry, to engage his blade with decision.'

" For my own part, I am quite satisfied that the system is a safe and sound defensive measure, which offers advantages that cannot be denied. Pressures, binds, beats and *croisés*, all those dangerous movements by which your opponent can bring the *fort* of his blade to bear on the *faible* of yours, are rendered very difficult to perform, and are much less likely to succeed. Surprise attacks are entirely or at least so nearly eliminated, that their occurrence is a rare event.

IV.

"I have endeavoured to state as clearly as possible the advantages that a weak fencer may derive from this system, when he is opposed to a combatant more experienced and more skilful than himself; but further than that, I believe that the skilful and experienced fencer has also something to gain by adopting this much despised method. I have myself never been able to discover that it is incompatible with perfect 'form,' or that it tends to wild play. It opens a wider field, it shows the fallacy of certain ideas, which have been wrongly supposed to be unassailable, and it furnishes a whole range of new situations, another world to conquer.

"What ground is there, I would ask my critic, for your assertion that I must be fencing blindly, because my sword does not happen to be in constant touch with yours? Why do you say that mutual hits must occur more frequently? If you are talking of a pair of duffers, who charge each other blindly, you may trust them to commit every possible blunder, whether they join blades or not.

"But why should you exalt so highly what

you call the faculty of touch, the power of judging the blade by touch, and be so ready to degrade that other sovereign principle, which may be called the faculty of sight, the power of judging the sword by eye? Can you deny the controlling influence of the eye, the authority that belongs to it? Do you believe that the eye cannot be trained to the same degree of nicety as the hand? Why, when you have these two forces at your disposal, are you content to let one of them do duty for both?

"You may keep your opponent at his distance by the menace of your nimble point, which flashes in his sight incessantly; while your watchful eye follows the movements of his sword and reads his thought, as well as if the blades were crossed and questioned each other by the language of the steel. Then, when it suits your convenience, when you see a favourable opportunity, when you have by a rapid calculation reckoned up the situation, weighed the chances, taken everything into account, then is the time to offer your sword, then is the time to engage your adversary, or by bold decided movements to get control of his blade."

V.

"But," objected one of my hearers, "what if your adversary adopts the same tactics, and refuses the engagement?"

"That is where science and strength, skill and personal superiority tell. What is fencing if it is not the art of leading your opponent into a trap, the art of making him think that he will be attacked in one place, when you mean to hit him in another? the skill to outwit his calculations, to master his game, paralyse his action, outmanœuvre him, reduce him to impotence?—That is the sort of thing the accomplished fencer sets himself to do.

"Your adversary, you say, will not come to an engagement. Very good; then you must force him to it by feints, or by threatening to attack. Either he attempts to parry or he attempts to thrust. In either case you get command of his blade by a simple or by a double beat, as the case may be, and then you drive your attack home.

"It holds good with fencing, as it does with all warlike measures, whether on a large scale or

small, that you must not wait for what you want
to be brought to you; you must learn to help
yourself; take no denial, but by force or fraud
get possession.

"Now, I appeal to you all as critics, not on a
technical question of fencing, on which no one
can be expected to give an opinion without a
thorough knowledge of the art, but on a simpler
matter. I will contrast two assaults. Imagine
that you are the spectators. The first is between
two fencers of the classical school, to use the
conventional phrase.

"The swords are crossed, and the two adver-
saries, both gifted with consummate skill, stand
facing each other, foot to foot. Feint follows
feint, and parry parry; a simple attack is
delivered, it is succeeded by a combination.
The attitudes of both are irreproachable; the
body always upright; the quick hand with
exquisite finesse manipulates the dancing point
by subtle and accurate finger-play. You admire
the exhibition; for a moment you follow the
quick passage of the blades, but your sympathies
are not aroused, you are not carried away, or
enthralled in spite of yourself in a fever of
anxious expectation.

"Now turn to the other assault. This also is fought by two skilful fencers, but they go to work on quite a different system.

"Look at the combatants. Instead of standing foot to foot, and blade to blade, they are out of distance, on the alert, ready to strike but cautious. Their eyes follow each other, and watch for the tell-tale movement. Suddenly they close, the blades cross, interlock, and break away. That was a searching thrust! But by a sudden retreat, a rapid movement, perhaps a leap backwards, the fencer evades the hit, and is ready on the instant to give back the point. This assault is a battle between two men, who mean hard fighting, keen swordsmen, dodgy, artful, and slippery, who bring to bear all their science, employ every trick they can think of, and throw themselves body and soul into the fight.

"Now let me ask you, which of these two assaults is the more interesting to follow?

VI.

" I remember an assault, in M. Pons's rooms, between one of my friends and a man who was generally considered and really was a strong fencer, although he insisted on clinging to that mischievous routine, which with some men is a superstition.

" They came on guard, and my friend, after crossing swords to show that he was ready to defend himself, quitted the engagement, attacked, and hit his opponent several times.

'But, Sir,' his opponent objected, 'you do not join blades.'

'Why should I ? '

' Unless you join blades, how am I to fence?'

'That is your look-out.'

' But you must join blades.'

'Why *must* I ?   My only object, I assure you, is to endeavour, as well as I am able, to disconcert my opponent, and as I find that this plan disconcerts you considerably, I see all the more reason why I should continue to employ it.'

'That may be,' rejoined the other sticking to his point, ' but if you do not join blades, it is not fencing.'

'Well,' said my friend, 'let us try for a moment to discuss the matter. Tell me, are my hits improperly delivered?'

'Oh, no.'

'Did I stab, or come in with a round-arm?'

'Certainly not.'

'Is there anything wrong with my parries? Are they too wide, or what? Is my hand too heavy, or do you complain of mutual hits?'

'No, that is not the point.'

'Then, what more do you want?'

'I want you to join blades.'

'To oblige you?'

'No, I do not say that. But unless you join blades it is not fencing.'

"And say what one might, nothing would make him budge from his everlasting axiom.

"It is always so, whenever an attempt is made to interfere with the traditions of any art whatever. The man who tries to strike out a new line cannot fail to disturb the tranquil repose of ancient custom. The conservatives resist, they object to interference, they feel that their placid triumphs, their cherished habits are threatened. The regular routine, which has been drilled into them, till they know it like an old tune of which every turn and every note is familiar, will be unsettled. They have good reason to be annoyed, but that does not prove them to be right.

VII.

"At the present day people have gradually come to admit that there is some good in these innovations, which have suddenly enlarged the scope of fencing. 'Fencing,' they say, 'is more difficult than it used to be, but less graceful.' Are these qualities then necessarily incompatible with each other?

"In order to make a clear distinction between those who run after strange gods, and the 'auld lichts' who have preserved intact the primitive tradition of the true faith, a phrase has been invented to describe the backsliders. They are said to be 'difficult fencers.'

"Now what are these words supposed to mean? Do they imply that a graceful fencer is not difficult? No doubt, classical grace and a masterly style are very fine things, which I, for one, can appreciate and admire. But if I am asked to choose between the graceful and the

c.   8

difficult fencer,—if it is not possible to be both at once,—I much prefer the latter, for I suppose that 'difficult' can only mean difficult to hit, difficult to defeat.

"But there is no need to suppose that difficulty is incompatible with grace, at least with grace of a certain kind, the grace of manly and robust energy, which sits well upon the fighting man, such grace as in old times so well became the gallant chevaliers, who illumined by their prowess the spacious days of ruff and rapier.

"We have here another of the important points of difference between the two schools. Some people treat the newcomer like an inconvenient guest, whom they cannot very well turn out of doors. But they may as well make up their minds that the intruder can take care of himself, and will find room for his ample proportions in the domestic circle. He has come to stay, and whether they like him or not he means to make one of the party.

"The axiom—'Hit and do not be hit back' ought, in spite of everything that can be said against it, to be the motto of all who fight with the sword. Science may teach how to hit well, but its first lesson should be, how not to be hit at all by the arrant duffer, who uses his sword by the light of nature. When swordsmanship fails to keep this end in view, we may be very sure that it is off the track. 'Business first' must be the invariable rule.

VIII.

"There was a time when the mask was not worn for the assault. And I remember reading some time ago in the *Encyclopaedia*, published about the middle of last century (1755), under the word *mask* the following remarks :—

'In foil-play Fencers have sometimes carried precaution so far as to wear a mask, to protect themselves from possible hits in the face. It is true that those who have acquired little skill in the Art may chance to wound their Adversary by a clumsy thrust, or cause themselves to be wounded by throwing up the point with a bad parry. It is however never worn at the present day.'

"This encyclopaedia evidently reflects the ideas which were generally accepted at the time.

8—2

To wear a mask in a bout with the foils was as much as to say that you considered your opponent a duffer, and was not far short of an insult.

" Fencing in those days was nothing but a formal series of attacks, feints, parries and ripostes, well understood and defined by the code ; every movement led up to some other movement, which was rigidly prescribed. If a fencer had ventured on a straight thrust while the feints were in progress, instead of elaborately following the blade through every turn of the labyrinth, he would have been considered an unmannerly cub, and sent back to study his rudiments. It was only in the last years of the period signalised by the famous Saint-Georges that the mask came into general use. Even then the only masks used were made of tin, and the professors' view was that such safeguards were permissible for rough players. But it so happened that three professors each lost an eye. And their respect for ancient tradition did not go far enough to induce them to risk losing the one that remained. After that the wire mask was generally adopted, but not without regret.

IX.

"Every generation takes the march of progress one stage further, or at least modifies
existing institutions in its own way. It is not
so long since the fanciful multiplication of feints,
of which I was speaking just now, was considered the correct game ; the right thing to do
was to follow the blade until you found it. At
the present day it is no longer part of the
necessary ritual to follow always every vagary.
Suppose you feint inordinately, I suddenly let
drive with opposition of the hand, or simply
straighten my arm and hit you with a stop
thrust, which interferes rather effectively with
your trickiness, and spoils the magnificent
flourishes of your arabesques. These hits are
now recognised and regularly taught. If need
be, instead of lunging you slip the left foot to
the rear, throw the left shoulder well back, so as
to be out of the way, and drop the body, in
order to avoid being hit yourself.

"The system of our fathers, which in many
respects was excellent but at the same time
was remarkable for several very odd and very

peremptory theories, has in many instances been successfully assailed. Perhaps in some cases its assailants have themselves been too peremptory, and this has led to that loss of temper and angry recrimination, by which the debate has been embittered.

"But I must not tax your patience further to-night. We had better adjourn the discussion until to-morrow; otherwise you will be tired of hearing me talk, and I am sincerely anxious to command your whole attention."

The Sixth Evening

A very old trick.

I.

" FENCING," I began, when we had all
reassembled as usual, " is such an in-
exhaustible topic, that I could not, if I would,
pretend to go minutely into all its practical
details. No one gifted with a modicum of
sense, a little determination, and a dash of
enterprise, can fail to strike out a line for himself.
I am obliged, as you see, to content myself with
a general view. For we cannot consider the
assault, and especially an assault in which the
combatants use their heads as well as their

hands, without assuming that our young friend has gained some science, and has become an educated fencer.

"I have already spoken of parries and ripostes, and you have seen that the lesson teaches how these should be employed. You know what use may be made of the sense of touch, the power of feeling the blade, and of the electric influence of the eye. It remains to say a few words on the subject of attacks.

"It is more dangerous to attack than to parry. Instead of waiting you let yourself go. And the great difficulty is to know how to let yourself go far enough without going too far.

"Remember that discretion is the better part of valour ; but do not confound discretion with timidity. I have already said that you ought to be able and willing, and more than that, that you ought to make it your object to encounter every sort of style, even those styles which are hardly worthy or—to be quite candid —are quite unworthy of the name. As a matter of fact there are such styles, and therefore it is just as well not to allow their exponents to become conceited, or to imagine that by any chance they can possibly be effective.

" It is important for the prestige of fencing, that those who have no knowledge of their weapon, or at most a mere smattering, should not be allowed to suppose that they can depend upon mere energy and a blind rush to defend themselves against a man who has been trained to the skilful handling of the sword. Confidence, that mainest mainstay of defence, ought not to be possible for the ignorant fencer; it ought to be the peculiar privilege of the trained and scientific expert.

II.

" To come back to the various situations which may occur in the assault. If I see a fencer, as soon as he falls on guard, engage swords, and at once hurriedly let fly thrust after thrust, attack following attack in quick succession, if he neglects to test the length of his opponent's sword by gradually feeling his way, by employing all the necessary tactics of the preliminary skirmish, by prospecting for information and discreetly sounding the enemy, then to my mind he may be classed at once. He may have some dexterity, a certain power of execution, but by the mere act of joining blades he may be set down as a blind fencer, far more truly than the man who keeps out of distance, and chooses the proper moment at one time to refuse, at another, when least expected, to take the engagement. or to seize his opponent's blade with courage and resolution."

" I suppose," remarked the Comte de R., " that, a few years hence, it is highly probable that a new set of theories will be invented to supersede these modern ideas, which are so hotly disputed now, and they in their turn will be considered out of date."

" No doubt that is to be expected in the nature of things. The form may or rather certainly will change, but the substance will be unaltered. Let me submit evidence to prove it. I mentioned the other day some old books on sword-play which I hoped to look through. I will only refer to them for one moment. I managed to read them all, and dreary reading it was, but I got through them, being supported by a conscientious sense of duty, and I unearthed among others the two following passages.

"The first on the subject of *Approaches* was written in the seventeenth century, that is to say, it is about two hundred years old :—

'The reason why you must make your steps of unequal Measure is that thereby you always hold your Adversary in Suspense and uncertain what you would be at. For if you always go about your business of a set way and with a set regularity of step, it may happen that the Enemy will make his reckoning so exactly, that he can direct his sword not only at the place where he sees you to be, but even at that place to which he knows you will presently come, whereof by this means he is hindered.'

"One might suppose that this was written yesterday. Could any professor, however skilful, put the point better or more logically? The weapons however were very different from ours, heavy cut and thrust rapiers, wielded sometimes in one hand, sometimes in both; but the laws of judgment, caution, and strategy were the same, and will be the same a hundred years hence.

"To prove once more that this new school, which a few years since was received with a howl of abuse, really did not advance such

very extravagant doctrines, and that the power
of eye, which we were discussing yesterday, is
intimately connected with the power of touch,
I have made a note of these other few lines,
still on the subject of attacks :—

' It follows that the great gain that Science
gives is Security in making your Approaches,
which cannot be obtained except you thoroughly
comprehend the Importance both of Touch and
Eye ; and you may rest assured that bodily
activity and readiness of hand are alike as
nothing when weighed against a good Approach.'

" And we are reluctantly obliged to admit
that after all our original ideas have been anticipated, and we stand convicted of plagiarism.

" I might revenge myself for the trouble I
have taken to ransack these ancient folios, by
inflicting upon you any number of quotations,
but I will be merciful, and am content to have
demonstrated that the ideas that are supposed
to be most radical are often, when they come to
be examined, most truly conservative."

III.

" I have another question for you," continued the Comte de R. "You were speaking the other day of feints and stop thrusts. Of course it was ridiculous to expect an opponent to follow every gyration, which you chose to describe with the point of your sword, but don't you think that nowadays the practice of straightening the arm on every possible occasion is utterly overdone?"

" No doubt it is by some men—overdone, or rather very badly done, which amounts to the same thing. '*Ne quid nimis*' you know is a good motto, and I quite agree with you, however little you may like it, that this movement, which comes more by instinct than by intention, is now the refuge of those who cannot parry ; but, mind this, it is a refuge, from which it is often very difficult to dislodge them. I quite admit that those who straighten the arm without any justification are hopelessly unscientific, but they present a difficulty to surmount, which requires serious attention.

" Let me explain before going on. There is a distinction to be made between stop thrusts, and time thrusts. The stop thrust is taken, when your opponent advances incautiously, or when he draws back his arm while executing a complicated attack, whenever in fact he makes a movement which leaves him exposed. The time thrust on the other hand, correctly speaking, is a parry of opposition,—the most dangerous of all parries, for if it fails it leaves you absolutely exposed and at the mercy of your opponent. I have seen it taught in the lesson by every master (as an exercise no doubt), but I have hardly ever seen a master put it into practice in the assault. The thrust has nothing to recommend it, but on the contrary it is to be condemned on many grounds. I should like to see it ignominiously expelled from the fencing room, as the buyers and sellers were expelled from the temple.

IV.

"Do you follow the distinction? A time thrust is taken on the final movement of an attack, when you think you know exactly what is coming, and can judge with certainty in what line the point will be delivered. Very well, then

parry instead of timing; for if you are wrong—
and who is not sometimes?—you can at any
rate have recourse to another parry. Whereas
the time thrust, when misjudged, results in a
mutual hit, and for one that is good tender how
much base metal you will put into circulation.
The stop thrust, which is taken, as I have said,
on the opponent's advance, is less dangerous.
Therefore never attack a man, who straightens
his arm on every occasion, without making sure
of his blade, and you need have no fear of the
result.

"It is quite true that the practice of straightening the arm is much more prevalent than it
used to be; simply because this style of play,
which is of great antiquity, had gone out of
fashion, and given place to another method,
which in its turn was overdone,—the method
of feints and flourishes.

"So too, the trick of reversing the lunge by
throwing back the left foot and dropping the
body, to allow the attack to pass over your
head, is not an invention of the 'Romantic'
school, as it has been ridiculously christened.
It is an old trick, a ruse of great antiquity,
which may or at all events ought to be found
in Homer. Still, unless your opponent drives

you to it by wild and frantic rushes, it is a
stroke to be used sparingly, and with the object
of letting him know that you are ready to receive him. By this means you will stop him
from rushing at you on every possible occasion.
I like to see a stop thrust correctly taken,
always provided that I do not see others in
the course of the same assault taken incorrectly,
—for then it is obvious that the correct thrust
was a simple fluke.

V.

"I am speaking now from the scientific
standpoint. Perhaps I can put my point more
clearly. If my opponent says :—'I don't profess
to be scientific ; I simply defend myself by the
light of nature,' he may do what he likes, I shall
not complain of his mistakes ; he is perfectly
within his rights and knows no better. But the
expert fencer has no business to make mistakes,
or at least he should try to avoid them as far as
he can.

"Even at the risk of being lynched for my
unorthodox opinions, I should venture to say to

the would-be fencer :—'Above all things make yourself dangerous. Be 'a difficult fencer,' since that is the stereotyped phrase. Without it there is no salvation ; your guns are not shotted, your performance is mere fire-works.'

"But be careful not to give these words a wider application than they are meant to carry. All that I would say is this :—that you are to follow your natural instinct, to trust your impulse, to be yourself and not your master's puppet. I do not mean to propound an acrobatic theory of fencing, or to recommend a meaningless, objectless, indiscriminate charging about, like the convulsive struggles of a wild beast, that has received its death wound. It would be as wrong to take such extravagant exceptions for your model, as it would be unfair to argue from them in order to demonstrate the futility of the new school.

"No doubt fencers of this kind,—they call themselves fencers,—may score an occasional hit, for, as I have had occasion to remark already, there is always a certain amount of luck in fencing; but this sort of thing is not fencing; it is much more like mere brutal fisticuffs. Such eccentric methods are of no importance, they are not based on any sort of principle, but are

9—2

the mere outcome of ignorance ; they belong to no school and have no permanent value. But it does not do to despise an unbeaten enemy. Therefore confront these methods and defeat them first ; you can afford to despise them afterwards."

"Quite so," exclaimed Monsieur de C., " that is exactly my opinion."

"One moment," I said, " I have not quite done. I was going to say, that I have very little faith in the stories one hears of the regimental fencing master being run through by the recruit. Such an event may happen, just as a chimney-pot may fall on your head when you are walking in the street, but I fancy that if you were to apply the rule of three to all the cases the result would not exactly support the paradox.

"There is a class of fencers who are thoroughly—in fact too thoroughly—convinced that they are very dangerous fellows, and that they are never hit. You repeatedly come across this sort of thing in the fencing room :—Your opponent delivers an attack which you parry ; he stays on the lunge doubled up, with his body dropped forward ; your riposte lands perhaps in his mask, perhaps in his back, or arm. Thereupon he recovers and remarks with a negligent air : 'hit in the mask,' 'hit in the back,' 'arm only,' as the case may be.

"Oh, only in the mask ! But, Sir, the point would have run you through the head and traversed your brain. In fact it would have been quite as effective as a hit in the chest, which penetrated your lungs. The other would have gone six inches into your back ; while the third would have pierced your arm and run you through the chest afterwards. You offer your head, back, or arm instead of your chest, I hit the part exposed and am quite satisfied. You cannot evade or parry a thrust by substituting for the part that would otherwise be hit some other part, which you do not attempt to cover ; all that you do is to offer an exchange.

VI.

"Do you suppose that these fencers would pursue the same tactics, if they had to face a naked point instead of the button of a foil, and that they would fancy themselves out of danger, if they laid themselves open to be run through the head or back or neck? Such wounds are not trivial and cannot be ignored. A sharp point is a peremptory fact, which makes short work of illusions.

"Or again, do you imagine that anyone would be very anxious in a real fight to run the risk of double hits, by which he might succeed in inflicting a serious wound, but only at the expense of being run through the body himself? No one would resort to such desperate measures as these, unless there was absolutely nothing else left to be done.

"This is so thoroughly true, that if you set two men to fight in a fencing-room with blunt swords, you notice at once that the assault is something very different from what it would have been with mere foils. You might almost fancy that the swords, though they can no longer wound, are still possessed by the spirit of mortal combat, and retain some reminiscence of the real thing, of naked chest opposed to naked steel.

"There is none of that brilliant dash, none of those brilliant strokes that are usually more conspicuous for temerity than judgment. The fight is a sham fight still, but the players cannot help taking it seriously. Each is saying to himself :—'Now let me see what would happen, if we were in earnest.' The different shape of the hilt, the harsh grating of the steel affect the imagination. 'Watch that fellow, see what he is up to, make him keep his distance, give him something to think about.' That is the sort of caution that the swords are whispering.

"You may easily satisfy yourselves of the truth of my remarks the next time you have an opportunity of watching a bout of this sort. And if there is so great a difference between simple foils and blunt swords, you will have no difficulty in believing that the difference between blunt swords and sharp is far greater. Wild play subsides, and those who were willing to charge blindly, when they risked nothing more than a dent in a leather jacket, prefer to study ways and means a little more closely. It is a very natural prompting of the instinct. The rule is almost universal, but there are occasional exceptions, which you may be called upon to face, and if you do not want to be taken by surprise, you had better make yourself acquainted with them beforehand for what they are worth."

"Then you approve," said M. de C., "of occasional practice with muffled swords?"

"Not only of occasional but of constant practice, and that not in the assault only, but in the lesson too. The greater weight of the sword and the wider blade, which is straight and less whippy than the foil, steady the hand, keep it in position, and give a truer aim."

VII.

"I notice," observed one of my friends, "that you have said nothing about left-handed fencers."

"No," I answered. "The fact is, there is hardly anything to say, and even the text-books, which do not usually err on the side of brevity, devote very little space to them. For there is really no particular rule, which applies to them exclusively."

"But surely they are very difficult?"

"Yes in a way no doubt they are, though one of my friends, a left-hander of course, used to say that the supposed difficulty is only a convenient excuse invented by right-handed fencers. His suggestion is more witty than true, and I am willing to allow, without hesitation, that left-handers really are puzzling to those who are not accustomed to fence with them. Their only real advantage is that they have more opportunities of fencing against right-handers, than right-handers have of fencing against them. When once you are used to them the difficulty vanishes. The left-hander on the contrary, when it comes to fighting, is never rid of the far graver risk which he takes by exposing his left side.

"I may add that the left-hander's advantage, which consists entirely in his incognito, would exist no longer, if the professors,—who I hope may take the hint,—would make a practice of giving lessons occasionally with the left hand. Some of them do so already, and I congratulate them on their good sense. If you come to think of it, there is not a single left-handed thrust or parry, which cannot be equally well executed by a right-handed player. Only, from want of practice, the latter finds it more difficult to direct his point because the lines are reversed. *Quarte* becomes *sixte,* and vice versa. The left-hander prefers to take the inside engagement, that is to say *quarte*. This line suits him better, and accordingly it is good policy not to let him take it without a struggle. It is usually more difficult to hit him in the outside line.

"So much for general principles, for of course left-handed play varies as much as right-handed, although the contrary is sometimes maintained. But if all left-handers were providentially made alike, one would think that it could not be very difficult to get to know the pattern by heart.

VIII.

"Well, you must admit that in the course of my remarks I try not to pass over anything that is likely to interest those who have, or those who should, could, or would have a fancy for sword-play.

"My object is to bring out the essential features in clear relief, and I intentionally omit the thousand and one minute details, which would overcrowd my canvas, and prevent you

from properly appreciating the leading features.
These refinements, which come with experience
and habit, cannot be forced, they must be slowly
acquired by the friction of the blades, by meeting all sorts and conditions of fencers, by facing
the unforeseen and sudden perils, which confront
you just when they are least expected.

"You know how awkward a young fellow is
when he makes his first appearance in society.
When he finds himself in a drawing-room, he is
shy and uncomfortable, he does not know how
to sit down or how to stand up or how to talk,
but presently without consulting any professor,
simply, so to speak, by the daily friction of his
common intercourse with other people, older
and more experienced than himself, he acquires confidence, ease, address, manners, and
so forth.

"It is just the same with fencers. Craft,
finesse, tact, and judgment come by degrees, as
wings grow out of feathers; but do not forget
that the lesson and the master's pad are your
first instructors and must not be neglected.
To neglect them would be ungrateful, and in-
gratitude is always base. Besides you cannot
afford it.

" I am sure I don't know what else I can
find to say ; I shall be in a difficulty to-morrow,
unless you promise to help me out."

A Stop Thrust.

The Seventh Evening

Toucher et ne pas l'être.

I.

"WELL, what is your text to-night?" asked my host as he joined the group which had met as usual in the smoking-room.

"Oh," I replied, "I have nothing left to preach about."

"And I," said the Marquis de G., who was looking through the evening paper, "don't mean to let you off so easily. Here is a piece of news, which is very interesting in connection with our nightly symposia."

"Read it! Read it!" exclaimed a chorus of voices.

The Marquis read out the following paragraph :—

'An unfortunate encounter recently took place in the Papal States between the young Marquis de Monte C. and the Chevalier d'A. The duel arose out of a very singular incident. The Chevalier d'A., a Neapolitan, has the reputation of a *jettatore*, that is to say he is supposed to have the evil eye. The Marquis de Monte C., happening to meet him in a drawing-room, took up without thinking a little coral hand, a charm that he was wearing on his watch-chain, and pointed it at the Chevalier d'A. as he was passing close by him. The Chevalier who knew what people thought of him, noticed the movement and called the young Marquis out. They met the following morning, and the unfortunate Marquis received a sword thrust in the chest and was killed outright. The Chevalier, besides being a very expert swordsman, is said to have acquired a knowledge of several secret thrusts.'

II.

The reading of this paragraph was followed by a momentary silence. Then someone remarked:—"I have often heard 'secret thrusts' spoken of, but how is it that they are not taught by the Professors?"

"Well," I said smiling, "for one sufficient reason, that if they were taught they would no longer be secret. But, joking apart, I may as well say at once that my belief in secret thrusts is about equal to my belief in ghosts."

"Come, this must be looked into."

"I believe in out of the way and unlooked for strokes, but further than that I cannot go."

"Yet, surely they must have existed some time or other," objected my critic, "or how did they come by their name?"

"Oh, they existed more or less at one time, or perhaps it would be nearer the mark to say that they were supposed to exist. They are a shadowy survival, a sort of family ghost that we have inherited from the Italian school. For French fencing, though it has developed characteristic features of its own, traces its descent, as you know, in a direct line from Italian ancestry.

"Secret thrusts died and were buried when
Science was in its infancy; and Science has
since grown up in other conditions, and grown
strong by working on other lines. They could
not be revived, unless the attendant ritual of an
effete tradition, the system of a bygone age
long since forgotten, were revived along with
them.

"At the present day, with our modern
weapons and our modern methods, to use a
secret thrust would amount almost to a crime.
And if it were not exactly that, if a charge of
murder or manslaughter would not lie, it certainly would be considered iniquitous by all
honourable men. No one with a conscience
could conceivably buy success in an affair of
honour at such a price.

III.

"Before we leave this question I should like
to make my meaning perfectly clear. In the
world as we find it there are some things for
which no definite penalty is prescribed, things
that do not bring a man within the law, but
that are none the less offences in the court of

conscience and very properly censured. An action, such as we are now discussing, is to my mind a case in point, always supposing it to be a possible action ; but is it possible ?—that is the question.

"Put yourself in the place of a man who is compelled by force of circumstances to fight a duel. Your success, if you do succeed, may be due to the blessing of Providence, to skill, or to accident, but it must satisfy one condition,—it must be unequivocal. You are meeting an honourable enemy in an honourable fight, and obviously the means you employ must be beyond all question 'straight,' and not devices so crooked as almost to deserve the epithet 'felonious.'"

I found myself speaking with some warmth, and was pleased to see that my remarks were received with great interest.

"Of course," I continued, "in speaking or writing on a subject of this sort, one can only express a strictly personal opinion. Now, what do you say ? We have been let in for this duel by an evening paper. Shall we drop it, or shall we see it through ?"

I was answered by a general cry :—"Go on !"

"I am afraid it may take us rather far afield, for it involves important considerations."

"So much the better," observed my host, "we have plenty of cigars, and the night is young."

We provided ourselves with fresh cigars to follow those already alight, and settled down in our arm-chairs, and the most profound silence reigned in the smoking-room.

IV.

"Well," I began, "hitherto we have had in view sword-play in the literal sense of the word, that is to say theoretical fencing, fencing regarded as a sport, as a bout with the foils in a fencing room.   We shall now have to consider it from the strictly utilitarian standpoint.

"In the one case we have an assault, consisting of a succession of fancy strokes played by connoisseurs, who in point of skill may of course be equally or unequally matched, but who nevertheless play the game on the whole in accordance with principles that are tolerably

well ascertained. In the other case we have a
serious encounter with swords sharply pointed,
flashing in the sun, and dangerous to life. The
first hit, correct or incorrect, is decisive, no
matter how it is delivered, no matter where.

"Do not forget that you have to reckon
not only with skill but with the possibility of
surprise, not only with subtlety but with brute
force, not only with science but with blind and
headlong ignorance. Your opponent does not
greatly care whether he lets your blood in
orthodox style, or whether he operates on your
face for instance, or on those parts of the body
that are too much neglected in the fencing room.
You do not choose your opponent, he is chosen
for you by accident; he may be tall or short,
strong or weak. You are no longer engaged in
a sport in which your object is to play correctly,
in a contest of skill in which you may perhaps
allow yourself to be hit occasionally in order to
lead your opponent on and afterwards defeat
him more easily. The man who confronts you
with that threatening point may be an artistic and accomplished swordsman, but he may
equally well never have touched a sword in his
life, and be trusting to luck, or to his general
smartness, or to a cool head. You may find

that you have to do with an enemy whose every movement is studied; who keeps his distance cleverly; who never advances or retires without a reason. Or on the contrary, it may turn out that your opponent, trusting to one supreme effort of audacity, in defiance of all calculation, and throwing to the wind every shred of theory, will make such brutal use of his sword as the primitive and untutored instinct of self-preservation dictates.

V.

"We realise at once how far we have got from the harmless diversion of the assault, the sham fight conducted under the master's eye on strictly correct principles and with inoffensive weapons. The assault and the duel are even further apart than the assault and the formal lesson. In short this newspaper paragraph has brought us face to face with the real duel, and what we have to do is to discuss it in all its bearings,—so we had better begin at the beginning.

"Unfortunately, one always finds that it is impossible to discuss the art of fence without coming to the duel; for say what you will, cases

must sometimes occur when an affront for which
the law offers no redress compels you to go out.
'The duel,' as someone puts it, 'cannot be sup-
pressed. It is like a bad neighbour with whom
we have to live on the best terms we can.'

"Some years ago I happened to read a great
deal of fencing literature. The various authors,
though not one of them could find a good word
to say for duelling, contrived between them to
fill in a sketch of its rise and progress from the
earliest times down to the present day.

"This is evidently one of the points where
the civilised man and the savage meet on common ground, and is an instance of the law that
civilisation modifies, refines, perhaps transforms
our instincts, dresses or disguises them in the
latest fashion, but never gets rid of them.

"At one time the duel was called Trial by
Battle or simply The Judicial Combat. Then
it was pronounced illegal, and those who fought
in a private quarrel were sentenced either to
death or to long and cruel periods of imprison-
ment.

"At a later period, growing insolent with
impunity, the duel like a strayed reveller swag-
gered in the streets and public places ; we find
it haunting the taverns, we see the flicker of the

blades under a street lamp,—drawn for a word, for a ribbon, for a bet, for anything, or for nothing. Even the seconds who parted good friends over-night did their best to spit each other next morning.

"Well, what better evidence could we require to prove that this last resort of wounded honour is somehow deeply rooted in human nature, than the fact that the ancient and honourable practice of duelling has remained the final court of appeal, in spite of changed surroundings, in spite of hostile opinion, and in spite of the extravagant follies that have sometimes disgraced it?

VI.

"But this is a digression for which I apologise. I was led astray by my subject and drifted quite unconsciously into an unpremeditated preface."

"Don't apologise," said M. de C., "your digression is charming."

"And besides," I continued, "you know I have a sort of moral claim on your indulgence, for I might have displayed my erudition, and

have quoted names and dates and facts unearthed from dusty folios, and yet I have
mercifully spared you."

"Oh, thank you, thank you!" came from
several arm-chairs.

"When one talks of duelling, there is a
point that strikes one at the outset, and though
it is not directly connected with sword-play, it
is too nearly allied to the duel to be dismissed
without notice. I mean the duties of seconds.

"I shall not now enter upon the question of
what those duties may be before the combatants
meet. These consist in pressing for moderate
counsels, in acting or even over-acting the part
of peacemaker. You all know as well as I do
that no chance of arriving at an honourable
settlement should be neglected before allowing
your men to go out.

"What should we think of the man who
could forget that his friend's honour and his
friend's life are equally committed to his keeping, and that he ought not, out of a quixotic
regard for the one, to jeopardise the other
needlessly?

"When a man fights, his conviction that
right is on his side is everything. And there-

fore the correct attitude of a second is that of a man, who acting calmly but firmly in his friend's interest seeks to avoid a quarrel. Any other attitude is not only incorrect but even renders him liable to be called to account for neglecting his bounden duty.

" Personally, if after exhausting every effort to obtain a friendly settlement I found that a meeting was unavoidable, although I was thoroughly satisfied in my own mind that it was a case not of injured honour but only of injured vanity, or of wounded pride, I should not hesitate to withdraw. Duels played to the gallery are either odious or absurd; they are out of date, and should be numbered with the obsolete fashions of the past.

VII.

" They arose in the manners and customs of a flamboyant era, when everyone carried a sword and it was considered the right thing to air it on every opportunity, in order to fill up the time which might otherwise have passed somewhat heavily. Every age has its fashions and its vices, its childish toys and favourite follies. Those gallant blades that cut such a tremendous figure in the old days would meet with a very poor reception now, if they could revisit the scenes of their dashing exploits.

"But if it is the duty of a second to play the part of mediator before the action, it is equally his duty to be cool and collected on the ground. His personal responsibility is increased, but otherwise his role remains unchanged.

"It then becomes imperative on him to anticipate and allow for every contingency, he must let nothing escape him, and must give the closest attention to the minutest detail, in order that his principal may be relieved of all anxiety, and may preserve that cool presence of mind which is so absolutely indispensable.

VIII.

"In short the fact that has to be grasped is simply this,—that not one of the thousand and one preliminary details is unimportant; and that things seemingly the most trivial may suddenly assume the most unexpected gravity. The stake is too high to justify any man in gambling it away with a light heart.

"In the first place the selection of the ground must be carefully considered. The surface should be smooth and even, without dips or inequalities that can be in the slightest degree dangerous. Be particular to avoid a spot where there is any grass. Grass is slippery and may imperil your friend's life.

"Here is another point worth remembering. Run your eye quickly but carefully over the ground where your friend will stand ; he is very likely to neglect this precaution himself, and may fail to see a root for instance, almost unnoticeable to a careless glance, which might very easily trip him up or throw him off his guard at a critical moment, when it was too late to stay the impetus of his opponent's point. All this no doubt seems extremely trivial ; but how do you know that the tuft of wet slippery grass, the half hidden root, or treacherous stone will not turn the scale a moment later ?

"The contending parties, it has been said, are entitled to a fair division of light and ground. If that is so, you will be well advised not to stand out for your share of light, and you should never consent to let your principal face the sun. The glitter of the blades confuses the eye and causes hesitation. Remember that in fighting the eye is an implement at least as important as the sword. Seeing in this case is thinking. The eye warns you of danger, and instinctively picks out the enemy's weak spot. And more than that, a steady eye, an eye that looks one in the face unflinchingly, overawes and fascinates. While the sword threatens, the spying questioning eye is the intelligent scout.

" Again, never allow the combatants to strip. The impression of the cold air on the bare skin and the unaccustomed exposure may affect one more than the other, if he is naturally more sensitive, even though he may be quite unconscious of the fact."

" But," objected the Comte de R., " what if the other side insist?"

"You must refuse to give way. No one has a right to insist upon it. It is a barrack-room practice, usual among soldiers, and does not hold good outside the guard-room."

IX.

" While we are on this point," remarked one of my friends, "there are two questions I should like to ask you."

"I will do my best to answer them," I replied, "for—as my lawyer would put it—I may say, that I am thoroughly acquainted with all the leading cases."

"Well, is it allowable to use a fencing glove?"

"It is usual. But custom is not always right, and though many men suppose that they are entitled to it as a matter of course, they cannot strictly speaking claim it. Generally the parties agree beforehand whether fencing gloves shall be used or not. It nearly always happens that both sides prefer to use them, for with the help of a fencing glove you get a firmer and more confident grip of the sword, and are less likely to be disarmed. Besides, the hilt of a sword is hard; it tires and bruises the hand; the fingers in contact with it are jarred at every parry that is at all strong, or whenever the blades meet sharply. On these grounds fencing gloves are generally allowed. However, if the seconds of one side object, the seconds of the other side cannot either require them to use a fencing glove or claim the right for their own principal.

"For instance, the objection may be raised that the use of a fencing glove is familiar to a man accustomed to fencing, but unfamiliar and of no value to one who has never fenced. True, this objection is seldom raised, because, as I pointed out just now, the man who is not used to fencing is of all men the one who finds a serious difficulty in handling the rough hilt of a sword, and who has everything to gain by using a padded glove.

"In any case you are at liberty to wear an ordinary leather glove, whether your opponent chooses to do so or not. Or you may wrap a handkerchief round your hand, to give you a firmer grip of the sword, provided you are careful not to leave a hanging end, which may dangle loose, and hinder the action of your opponent's point."

X.

"I will now put my second question," continued my inquisitor.

"Well, what is your second question?"

"Is it permissible to use the unarmed hand to parry and put aside your opponent's blade?"

"Oh! that is a very serious matter, which I did not mean to pass over in silence. But it involves the consideration of several points,

which would perhaps take us too far to-night.
Suppose we leave it for to-morrow."

"Then we adjourn until to-morrow," said
the Comte de C.

And so we broke up.

The Eighth Evening

A Parry with the hand.

I.

"YOU asked me yesterday, if it is allowable to use the unarmed hand to parry and put aside the sword.

"My answer is very emphatic:—No."

"But what if the parties agree to allow it beforehand?" asked the Marquis de R....

"That is an agreement which in my opinion ought not to be made. The practice is wholly foreign to our ways and to the traditions that have come down to us.

"I am fully aware of the fact that there is the authority of a very profound writer, the Comte de Chatauvillard, who has many strong supporters, for the statement that 'the parry with the hand may be a matter of agreement.' And other writers, among whom is more than one eminent master, may be quoted for the view that it is a proper matter for arrangement between the contending parties. That does not affect my opinion in the least; and I say very emphatically and very distinctly : — As you clearly have the right to say yes or no, say no invariably.

"Such a concession or such an agreement, even if it is freely entered upon by both sides, is only too likely to lead to disastrous and fatal mistakes, while it does not offer any counterbalancing advantage. I will try to explain why.

"The parry made with the hand that does not hold the sword goes back to the ancient traditions of the Italian school, to the methods in vogue when men fought with sword and dagger. They parried and attacked with either weapon indifferently, bringing one or other into play by voltes and passes, which have been dismissed from the theory and practice of modern fencing. The art, which was adapted in those days to the double means of offence and defence, employed a system very different from that which prevails now. This parry, or to speak more accurately this method of diverting an opponent's blade, which was done with either hand indifferently, was reasonable then ; nowadays it would be a fantastic and dangerous anomaly.

"I remember trying by way of experiment, some years ago at Naples, several assaults of this sort with an Italian professor, named Parisi. —The poor fellow died I believe in prison, after taking part in one of the many revolutionary attempts that were made to wreck the kingdom of Naples. Parisi used to come regularly to my house where I had furnished a room for fencing. I wished to make a serious study of Italian play, and of the surviving traditions of this school, which is rapidly disappearing and is only connected with its past by a few almost invisible threads.

"Well, Parisi used to fence with a long Italian sword in one hand, and in the other a sort of stiletto, which he employed to parry my attacks in certain lines; and while he thus stopped my attack with his dagger, he made not exactly a riposte but rather a simultaneous counter-attack on me with his sword. This kind of play, which continually produced new and difficult situations, was very interesting.

"If Parisi dropped his dagger, what happened? His left hand, instead of following my blade, sprang at once to a fixed position. And to what position? Why, you could see at a glance, by the way he carried his forearm, thrown rather high across his chest and only a few inches away from it, that he was ready for the parry with the hand, in fact doubly ready for it, both by the position of his body and by the forward position of his left arm.

"Now we who follow the rules of French fencing do just the reverse. We carry our left arm to the rear, and so leave a smaller surface exposed to our opponent's point; we therefore cannot bring our left hand into play without abandoning the French position, or at all events without sacrificing some of its fundamental principles.

II.

"It is a good many years since I first took up fencing; I have been in all the fencing-rooms; I have fenced with many professors and with all sorts and conditions of amateurs, and no one has ever suggested to me that we should agree to parry with the hand. I have never, no not once in all the assaults that I have witnessed, heard such a suggestion made; I have never seen this kind of parry employed; I have never heard of a master showing or teaching it to his pupils as a possible case or even as a highly improbable case, against which it was his duty, as a wise and experienced professor, to put on their guard those whose instruction was committed to his care.

"Then why, when the assault ceases to be an exercise or an amusement, why, when you stake your life upon the issue, should you go out of your way to suggest or assent to something foreign to all recognised practice?

"If you approve of the surviving methods of the old Italian school, you should admit all the precepts of that school, and then you will at least be logical.

"Your sword will have a long heavy blade, broad and perfectly rigid; the hilt will be surmounted by a little cross-bar of steel on which you will place your fingers, and to which you will attach them with a long ribbon; incidentally you will do away with the freedom of the hand, the supple action of the wrist and the niceties of finger play. You will have to make frequent use of parries of contraction, which are indispensable to Italian play, though they are little valued, not to say altogether ignored by the French school. You must learn your voltes and passes, the manoeuvres of ducking and dodging; and then, I repeat, you will at least be logical. But an agreement which recognises only one of these practices, while it disregards all the rest, seems to me absurd.

"Let me now show you the danger, which can hardly be avoided, of admitting this parry with the left hand.

"Between the open palm, which merely

brushes the blade aside, and the hand, which by
a nervous movement closes unconsciously on
the blade and holds it fast, the difference is
very hard to seize. The thing is done in a
moment. It passes like a flash in the confusion
of the encounter and leaves no trace behind.

"Without a doubt the man who has unconsciously arrested the blade, instead of merely
turning it aside, will be in despair, and in the
loyalty of his heart will be the first to accuse
himself. But if his point has taken effect, if he
has delivered a fatal thrust, will his despair or
regret or any self-reproach heal the wound that
he has inflicted, or restore the life that he has
taken? If the odds were a thousand to one
against a fatal issue, that one chance would
be enough to condemn fatally this dangerous
agreement.

"Moreover, I may remark, speaking from the
experience that is obtained by long familiarity,
and perhaps from some small skill in the practice
of arms, that it is often very difficult, not to say
impossible, for the most practised eye in the
confusion of a multitude of thrusts, swiftly
parried and as swiftly returned, to follow with
accuracy the course of two swords, that pass to

and fro and interlace like living things, or to judge with indisputable certainty the difference between these two movements, one of which is authorised by consent, while the other may suddenly turn an honourable fight into a foul assassination.

"The mere act of judging so bristles with difficulties, that it is likely to lead to a conflict of opinion between even the most unbiassed judges. Who can decide between them? The fact on which their judgment is based is there no longer. It passed in a moment, quick as thought. Consider the terrible position in which you are placed, in the presence of a man lying stretched on the ground before you, cold and lifeless, who ought to be a living man full of strength and vigour.

"And now, I appeal to all seconds. In the name of good sense, in common fairness, could you or could you not with a clear conscience take the heavy responsibility of such a risk?

III.

"I am trying, you see, to obtain a comprehensive view of the manifold duties of seconds, and to omit none of the minute matters of detail, which it is their duty to attend to, and which ought to be present to their minds. Here is another point, which is worthy of their serious attention.

"When the combatants have taken sword in hand and the blades are crossed, the seconds should stand within reach, holding a sword or walking-stick, and ready to stop the fight should any irregularity occur, or if either of the men should slip, or stumble, or be disarmed, or wounded. This last case especially requires their utmost vigilance, for there are two events, both equally disastrous, that may occur.

"Suppose one of the men is wounded. In the natural excitement of the moment, the man who has delivered the thrust is often unaware that his point has taken effect. Before he can tell that his opponent is disabled, perhaps before he can check himself, he may inflict a second wound, unless the swords are instantly knocked up.

" The wounded man, on the other hand, may not immediately feel the effect of his wound, and by continuing to fight may run the risk of being wounded a second time, and that more seriously. It may also happen, and this is the great danger, that in a fit of blind rage he will rush madly on his opponent.

" Again, the man who has inflicted a wound and has felt his point go home, instantly and instinctively stays his hand, and even if his opponent renews the attack hesitates to strike a second time one who is already hurt. It is during this juncture of a moment's pause with a moment's hesitation that the wounded man may make his mad rush, and either run his opponent through the body, or meet his own destruction, if his opponent has promptly recovered his guard, and calmly offers him his point.

IV.

"Both cases are alike disastrous, for either may lead to a fatal result at a time when by the wound already received the fight may be regarded as closed, or at least as suspended. The seconds, who by redoubling their precautions might have saved the useless shedding of blood, will of course be held to blame.

"No doubt it sometimes happens that in spite of the closest attention the attack is so prompt, so impetuous, so swift, that it is impossible to intervene in time. But then at all events the seconds will have no cause for self-reproach. Fortunately such cases are of very rare occurrence, but they do sometimes happen ; and it is therefore very necessary for the seconds to watch the crossed swords incessantly, and to follow their every movement, in order to intervene the moment that one of the men is wounded, however slight the wound may seem.

"If on examination the wound is found to be so trivial that the fight can continue without disadvantage to the wounded man, the com-

batants will at least have had time to recover
their coolness and self-possession.

"This close attention is one of the most
important points; it is in fact a matter of
absolute necessity. Here is the seconds' real
difficulty, for here the whole responsibility rests
with them.

"I have still several things to say, of which
you will recognise the importance. But it is
getting late, and if you will allow me I will
postpone them to our next meeting."

The Ninth Evening

Corps à Corps.

I.

" I wish," remarked the Comte de C..., when we met the next day, "that you would tell us what you think of the *corps à corps* in the duel."

"That," I replied, "is the very thing I was going to talk about."

"The right course in my opinion is to come to an agreement with the seconds of the other side that the combatants shall be separated and start afresh, when they become entangled at close quarters in what is termed a *corps à corps*. Otherwise, in a struggle of this sort it is impossible to

C.

say what may happen, except that both men are likely to receive their quietus,—a very symmetrical settling of their accounts by the process of double entry.

"But here again, one cannot help feeling that we have another thorny case, which calls for the exercise of judgment with due regard to the circumstances of the moment and fair play for both sides.

"If one of the men makes a furious rush on the other, the seconds ought not to knock up the swords until the man who has stood the attack has delivered his riposte. For he has gained this clear advantage, that after stopping the rush he is prepared with an effective rejoinder, and this advantage he is clearly entitled to use.

"Many questions of duelling must be left to the impartial discretion of the seconds. There is therefore no need to consider what would happen, if a second were to take unfair advantage of an agreement, honourably entered into on both sides, by interfering when the case expressly provided for had not arisen."

"Well, but suppose such a thing did happen?"

"Why, then, your conscience must tell you how to act. Perhaps you might interfere summarily to stop the proceedings, if the nature of the quarrel allowed it, or you might call upon the second who had so misconstrued his duty to withdraw and take no further part in the affair.

" I have often heard men say :—' If I were acting second in an affair that was not so serious as to warrant a fatal issue, and were to see that my principal was about to be run through the body by a thrust that would certainly be fatal, I should not hesitate to knock up the swords. I could not resist the temptation ; my feelings would be too strong for me. And as a matter of fact should I be very far wrong ? '

" Yes, my friend, you would be absolutely wrong. You would be assuming the most onerous, the most terrible responsibility, and your action, though dictated by a praiseworthy impulse, would probably cause you the most bitter remorse.

" For consider :—you have arrested the sword which would have struck one of the opponents full in the body. The fight continues, and the man whose blow you intercepted with the praise-worthy motive, I quite admit, of preventing a mortal wound, is himself wounded or possibly

killed. Fortune which favoured him at the outset suddenly turns against him and favours his
opponent, perhaps with a lucky fluke, a thing
which no foresight can prevent. What would
your feelings be, when you saw stretched at
your feet a man whose death you had caused
by exposing him to a danger that he ought
never to have encountered?

"A duel is always a miserable business; but
when once you have faithfully and energetically
done all that you can to prevent it, you must
leave chance to decide between the combatants;
only see that you take all the measures that are
in your power to minimise the chances of a fatal
issue."

"It seems to me," someone remarked, "that
if, when a friend asks you to oblige him with
your services, one were to think of all these
innumerable responsibilities, one would invariably decline to act."

"I don't know whether one would always
decline, but I know very well that the second's
part is one of unsparing self-sacrifice and devotion. I know that the man who undertakes it
lightly cannot be too severely blamed, and I

may add that I have never accepted the charge without passing a sleepless night haunted by the most gloomy forebodings. The second who conceives that he is merely required to be a passive witness, robs the part of all its meaning, all its value, all its dignity.

"You remember, I was speaking just now of the case of a second who acting on the spur of the moment instinctively intercepts a blow. I will give you an experience of my own.

"I was once acting for a friend in an affair of honour; I was thoroughly on the alert and carefully following the play of the points with that close attention, and perhaps I may say with that sureness of eye, which one acquires from some familiarity with sword-play, when I saw the opponent's point coming straight at my friend's body. Before I could think, I saw in an instant, as no one accustomed to fencing could fail to see, that the wound would be mortal. I knocked up the swords, and as the two men had got to close quarters, I called out :— 'On guard.' But I had hardly done so, when I realised the full extent of my unconsidered action, and I felt—well, I really cannot tell you what my feelings were at that moment. Luckily for me, my friend, who was no less clumsy than brave, was not the man to leave me long in this cruel position. He fell a few seconds later seriously wounded.

"The simple fact is, that where so many considerations have to be taken into account, you cannot be too careful never to go a step beyond the limits of strict and unassailable justice, in fairness to yourself and to everyone else concerned.

II.

"In this connection I am reminded of another case, which not unfrequently occurs, and on which I have sometimes heard the most contradictory opinions expressed, for it presents a really difficult problem.

"In the course of the fight one of the antagonists calls for a halt—have you the right to insist that the fight shall continue without interruption?

"In my opinion you unquestionably have that right, unless the case has been already provided for, or both men consent."

"Still surely," said the Comte de C..., "in a

prolonged set-to, if your opponent is exhausted,
if he is so done that he can hardly hold his
sword, if he is blown and distressed, you cannot refuse to give him a minute or two to
recover his wind."

"Well," I replied, "I have stated what I
believe to be the rights of the case, on which
either combatant can fairly insist. I will now
give you my reasons.

"Your opponent, you say, is done; well,
perhaps he may be, but have you considered
why? Is not his fatigue due to the violence
and the excessive energy with which he began
the fight, to the regardless eagerness with which
he has assailed you, without consulting his staying powers or husbanding his strength? You
have had to bear the brunt of all this fury, you
have sustained incessant attacks, but you with
more skill have economised your resources and
have bided your time to attack him. That
opportune moment evidently comes just when
your opponent, exhausted by the failure of his
repeated attacks, is likely to offer you the least
resistance.

"Then what happens? He calls for a halt!
And are you to let him off without pressing the

advantage that you with your judgment and
self-restraint have held in reserve? Are you to
give him leave to recover his wind, that is to
say to recover his strength and rally his scattered
forces, in order that he may start afresh to make
a second onset with the same ardour and the
same violence as before? The danger that
you have safely encountered once may prove
too much for you the second time. How does
that strike you? Surely it is as though a man,
engaged in a duel with pistols, in which each
party is at liberty to fire when he chooses, were
to be in too great hurry to let fly at his opponent,
and then, when his barrels were emptied and
useless, were to ask permission to reload, before
he has received his opponent's fire.

III.

" Situations requiring nerve and self-control
undoubtedly occur in a duel with pistols, but
similar situations, more trying and more critical,
occur in a duel with swords. You are willing to
admit them in the one case, yet you refuse to
admit them in the other."

" But, after all," persisted my critic, " you can
hardly strike a man, who is so utterly done that
he can hardly keep his point up."

" Quite true; but do you feel that hesitation,
when you raise your pistol to fire on a man who
has emptied his barrels? Do you not say, and
with perfect justice, 'I have stood his fire, it is
his turn now to stand mine'? Yet the cases are
strictly parallel. In each case you have taken
the risk and have escaped unhurt, and the
empty pistol in your opponent's hand is more
completely spent than a sword in a hand that
is nerveless from fatigue. For no power can
recharge the pistol with the ball that has sped,
but on the contrary a man with a sword in his
hand may possibly by a supreme effort pull himself together, and dangerous to the last strike
you before you can strike him.

" But here, as usual, fashion refuses to be
logical, and the sentiment of chivalry, which
we look for in all right-minded men, does not
nowadays allow us to make use of an advantage,
which some day or other, perhaps in precisely
identical circumstances, may very likely be
claimed without scruple.

IV.

"There is, by the way, another argument which I remember was once put to me by a friend, and which struck me forcibly at the time.

"My friend, who is something of a scholar, and has not forgotten his Latin, quoted these lines from Virgil :—

Ille pedum melior motu fretusque iuventa ;
Hic membris et mole valens ; sed tarda trementi
Genua labant, vastos quatit aeger anhelitus artus[1].

"These verses describe the fighting qualities of two heroes, who are about to enter the ring.

"No one, I suppose, would seriously maintain that they ought to be handicapped, that one of them should be made to concede some points in which he is superior, that is to say some of the chances in his favour, while the other retains all that he can muster. And yet can we not easily imagine two men meeting to fight a duel, one of whom has in his favour every chance but

---

[1] Dares the nimbler-footed, in manhood's confident ease;
Huge Entellus of limb and of weight,—but his tardier knees
Totter, and troubled breath convulses his towering frame.

VIRGIL, *Aeneid* v. BOWEN.

one, advantage of reach, dexterity, speed, and swordsmanship, while the other relies only on sound condition and great staying power?

"In an unequal combat such as this, what can the latter do but tire his opponent out, get him thoroughly well blown, and so reduce the balance of advantage, which until then tells with full force against him? The other man who thereupon calls for a truce is practically asking his antagonist to forgo his superiority of sound wind and limb, while he, so far from giving up his own advantages of reach, dexterity, and science, has every intention of making the most of them when the fight begins afresh.

"Then again, the staying power which you handicap, is very likely derived from a well developed chest which incidentally offers a larger target to the adverse point; the greater vigour may be due to the fact that its owner is thick-set, with heavy muscular limbs which make his movements slow and ponderous. Why recognise the inequality of the match in the one case, and disregard it in the other?

V.

"Suppose, added my friend, that the question is discussed by the seconds before the fight begins. One side might say:—'If our man is tired or blown, you will have no objection, we presume, to allowing a short interval?' 'We cannot agree to that,' the other side would reply. 'The only chance we have of making an even fight of it is that our man should outstay yours.'

"If they insist, the answer is this:—'Your man has every acquired advantage, ours has only the one advantage of superior physique. If we are to give up our points, you must forfeit yours, and how can you?'—Some arguments are so one-sided.

"In conclusion, I think that such questions may very properly be debated between the seconds, but that they ought never to come to the ears of the principals, for one of them might seem to be asking a favour, which the other would have a perfect right to refuse.

"I feel that I have dwelt on this matter at great length, but I was anxious to sift it thoroughly, because it is of vital importance and has often given rise to a serious conflict of

opinions. I have tried to give you the rights
of the case in a strictly impartial spirit. Exceptional cases may occur, to which the rule cannot
be applied without hardship, but such circumstances, as for example the bad health or feeble
constitution of one of the combatants, should be
provided for by arrangement."

VI.

"One more question, please," continued the
Comte de C., "just to complete my cross-
examination. When a man is called out, can
he be required to fight two duels with two
opponents in succession?"

"No, that cannot be expected of him. The
man who has fought once ought to be treated
as a privileged person, and cannot in any case
be compelled to cross swords a second time.
Tired as he is, or as he may be by the first
encounter, he stands at a disadvantage in meeting a fresh antagonist. A second encounter, if
it cannot be avoided and if both sides consent,
ought not to take place until the next day, or
after an interval of at least some hours, unless

the party interested, that is to say the man who has already fought, requests that it may take place at once.

"But on no account should the man, who at a later stage may probably or possibly become a principal, witness the first encounter either as a simple spectator or as a second. For the mere fact of his presence gives him a real and indisputable advantage, especially if the duel is fought with swords. And then the first law of the duel,—that it should be a fair fight with no favour,—is broken.

"There is one case and strictly speaking only one, in which his presence is permissible. That is, when being the party injured and therefore having the choice of weapons he selects different weapons from those employed in the first encounter,—pistols for example, if the former fight was with swords, or swords if it was fought with pistols. But, I repeat, this can only be allowed, if the man who has already fought wishes it or consents to it freely. In any other circumstances if I were acting second on an occasion of this sort, I should refuse to countenance a duel which I should consider equally irregular and unfair.

VII.

"Take the question on its merits. In a duel
with swords there are two things you want to
know : first, what is your opponent's natural
temper, when he is fighting in earnest; secondly,
what is the character of his play and the quality
of his swordsmanship. No one can deny that it
is very advantageous to know, whether the man
that you have to face is impatient and excitable
or self-possessed and cool ; whether he will
attack you with resolution or play a waiting
game ; whether he will attempt to parry or
simply offer his point ; whether he is energetic
or the reverse, skilful or clumsy, an ugly cus-
tomer or not particularly formidable. The fact
of your presence at a previous encounter is
sufficient by itself to give you information on all
these heads. You are reassured and reinforced;
undisturbed by doubt and hesitation you can
mature your plans at leisure with a quiet mind.
You have been over the ground and know how
the land lies. Even if you have not the vaguest
notion of fencing, if your ignorance is so complete that you are not in a position to make the
best use of all this valuable information, still the

fact that you have been a spectator of the first
fight, apart from any conclusions you may draw,
robs of its imaginary terrors the great unknown,
and shows you what you have to do.

"Your antagonist on the contrary has everything to learn.   He does not know whether you
are skilful or incompetent; whether he ought to
attack you or to wait for your attack; whether
your nerves are shaky or firm ; whether you are
naturally cool or excitable.   He is in the dark
a stranger feeling his way in a new country.
You, meanwhile, having no need to waste time
on such deliberations, go to work at once, with
every probability of winning an easy victory.

"Therefore, just as in the case of the man
who is at a disadvantage in point of science and
practice, but superior in bodily strength, sound-
ness of wind, and condition, I maintained that
he has as much right to make full use of those
advantages as his opponent has to use those
which he possesses, so in the situation we are
now considering, I maintain that we must refuse
to allow anything that goes to handicap the
combatants, or tends to incline the scales un-
fairly on one side rather than the other.

"It may be that some of the considerations,
that I have put forward, have not occurred to

you before. But now, bearing them in mind, can you say that you really and truly believe that such a fight as this is a fair fight, or that you would consent to have anything to do with it?

"I think that I have said everything that I had to say on the duties of seconds, as they appear to me in the light of my own experience and of the history of the subject. To-morrow we will discuss a still more important matter, the methods to be adopted by the principals."

The Tenth Evening

The instinctive position.

I.

THE next day found us lighting our cigars as usual. Brilliant conversation, you know, cannot be maintained without something to smoke. Our talk this evening was to be about the methods of attack and defence, which offer the most likely chances of success in an actual duel.

I began at once:—"Yesterday," I said, "I was speaking of the whole duty of seconds. I endeavoured to describe as clearly and fully as

possible, what they ought to do and provide for,
and I showed why it is essential that they
should follow every stage and every incident
of the fight with the utmost keenness, for the
onus of responsibility is rightly held to rest on
them.

"The preliminaries are now settled; the
antagonists, armed with swords of equal length,
stand face to face. One of the seconds is
stationed between them. He addresses to each
in turn the venerable formula:—'Are you
ready?—On guard.' Upon their assenting he
steps back and gives the fatal word:—'Go.'

"The fighting is about to begin, and the two
men stand expectant, neither stirring yet, each
sheltering his life behind a few inches of cold
steel.

II.

"There are only three contingencies that
we need consider, which naturally divide the
discussion under three heads. The first arises,
when a man who has never touched a sword
finds himself opposed to an old hand. The

second, when both antagonists are alike un-skilled. The third, when both are adepts.

"I may say at once with regard to this last case, that in a duel between two skilful opponents the advantage of superior science which one or the other of them may possess vanishes more often than not, and is compensated for by difference of temperament. For I cannot remind you too often, that in actual fighting it is not a question of hitting your opponent often, or of placing your point artistically, but of striking somehow and anyhow one blow and only one.

"Swords are not worn now, and swordsmanship as a necessary part of polite education has gone out of fashion. Our more punctilious ancestors prided themselves on never wounding their antagonist except with some thrust ingeniously conceived and brilliantly executed. Perhaps it was better so. It was certainly more picturesque, more chivalrous and magnificent. To mistake your sword for a spit, though you might succeed in running your antagonist through and through, would have been voted a blackguardly proceeding, unworthy of a gentleman. Molière's principle is good enough for us :—'*Hit the other man, and don't be hit your-*

self.' Our object is to hit no matter where,—no matter how. The art of fence is now so much neglected that it seldom happens when two men go out to fight, that they have even a passable knowledge of their weapon.

III.

"When a man knows nothing about fencing, either because he has never touched a sword, or because he has only knocked about with his friends in a rough way and very occasionally, his first thought when he has to fight is to call on a professor, and endeavour to obtain some ideas which will enable him to defend himself on the field of battle. I will describe one of these lessons which the professor is expected to give, and I shall try to point out the only sort of advice that is of universal application in such cases.

"The novice explains that he has to go out the next morning, and requests the professor to be good enough to give him a hint or two.

'Do you know anything about fencing?' enquires the professor.

'No, practically nothing.'

'You know that one holds the sword by the hilt and tries to hit the other man with the point, and that is about all, I suppose,' continues the professor, who will have his little joke. And he takes down a pair of swords provided with buttons, hands one to his pupil, and the lesson begins.

"One wonders how often this same lesson has been repeated. It never varies, and it never ought to vary. Its whole value lies in its simplicity.

"The ignorant fencer can do nothing without a cool head and steady nerve, which are the more effective, when they are opposed, as they often are, to bluster and over-confidence.

"First and foremost the professor must make his pupil understand the absolute necessity of standing firmly on his feet with an easy balance that allows perfect freedom of movement. The position, whatever it may be, that your extempore pupil falls into naturally, is the position you must accept. It is important to give him confidence in it and to modify it only so far as is absolutely necessary to enable him to move about easily. Your business is to make the best of this position, and if possible turn even its defects to account.

"The body should be inclined forwards rather than backwards. In this somewhat crouching attitude the upper part of the body, that is to say the chest, by its advanced position with the sword arm held in front, acts as a kind of natural rampart or shield to cover the lower part, where a wound is almost certain to prove mortal.

"Keep in view from the very first the importance of inspiring confidence in the unpractised fencer. For confidence alone implies some sort of self-possession and reacts immediately on nerve and muscle. He soon begins to feel somewhat more at ease. Some slight modifications are all that is required to correct the glaring faults that are most obviously dangerous.

"I am not afraid of putting the truth of my statement to a practical test. If you will now, all of you, take one of those swords which I see hanging on the wall and place yourselves on guard, not in what you imagine to be a fencing attitude, but as you would stand if you were seriously threatened, you will find that the attitudes you assume will all be very much alike, apart from such slight variations as are due to differences of physique."

IV.

" Come, I'll be your shocking example," said one of my hearers. " I have never touched a sword in my life. See what you can make of me."

" Very good," I replied, rising as I spoke ; and taking down a pair of swords I handed him one. Then without giving him time to think, I made a quick movement and threatened him with the point.

Instinctively he threw himself on guard.

" There, that will do," I said, " stay as you are ; I only wish you could be photographed to illustrate the instinctive attitude. Oh, don't be too conceited ; I do not mean to say that your position is faultless,—very far from that ; but the attitude in which you are standing is the origin of the orthodox guard as taught in the

fencing-room, because it is essentially the attitude that accords with our natural fighting
instincts."

"I am getting tired of this," observed my
patient, who had scrupulously stuck to his
position.

"One moment," I replied. "You are tired
because your arm is too much extended. Draw
it back a trifle, to relax the muscle and give
them their natural play. Carry yourself more
upright by slightly raising the body. Your left
foot is too far from the right; bring it rather
more forward; sink down a little on your legs,
so as to be ready either to spring quickly to the
rear or to advance.

"Bring your right shoulder forward, in order
to expose your chest less, but not further than
you can manage with comfort. You see I am
not very exacting.

"There, that will do very well.

"Now, if I make a movement, straighten
your arm boldly, and step back.

"Very well done.

"And yet you tell me you have never touched
a sword, or even a foil in a fencing-room. Then

all I can say is that I could not have chosen a
better subject for my demonstration.

" We will now put the swords back in their
place, and return to our discussion. Perhaps I
may have occasion to trouble you again by and
by."

" I am entirely at your disposal, Professor,"
replied my obliging pupil.

V.

" The rest of the lesson may be summed up
in a convenient formula. For so far as I know,
there is only one really useful tip that a professor
can give to the uninstructed novice who says :—
' This afternoon or to-morrow morning I have
to go out.'

" The professor will make a great mistake if
he attempts to teach him some fancy stroke, for
he will only disturb the natural working of his
instinct, without controlling it. He must remember that the excitement of fighting does
not leave much room for thought, and he must
accordingly take care to limit his instruction to
the simplest and clearest ideas, easy to understand and easy to put into practice, such as arise

naturally out of the instinctive sense of self-preservation.

"These remarks of course do not apply to those dull and inert creatures, cursed with a temperament so heavy, and so sluggish, that they do not know what it is to move briskly and can never rise to the occasion. You can put nothing into such as these and can get nothing out of them.

"When swords are crossed, the thing to do is simply what our friend here did just now :—Retire. I say 'retire' in order to avoid saying 'run away.' Retire always, retire incessantly, but retire little by little, so as not to consume once and for all the entire *hinterland* ; retire in short, not like a man in a panic, but like one who is watching his opportunity.

"Never forget this,—the only principle that at the critical moment is available for him who cannot count on science to assist him :—*Get back and straighten the arm ;*—or in other words :—*Defend yourself by threatening your opponent.* Never attack ; that is the point on which your attention must be concentrated."

"But," exclaimed one of my hearers, "what do you mean by 'threatening?' It is not so easy to threaten when you are an absolute duffer."

VI.

"The naked point of a sword resolutely offered at the body or at the face is always a threat. No one who sees it directed straight at him with a set fixity of purpose and a suggestive glitter can fail to be alarmed by it or can afford to disregard it, more especially perhaps if he knows that the man behind it is unsophisticated, and cannot be depended upon to obey the ordinary rules, that he has no deep design or artful scheme in the background, but just one idea—to keep his point always there, like a sentry at his post.

"Put shortly, my advice amounts to this:— Defend yourself by retreating ; threaten by offering the point. Offering the point, that is to say straightening the arm, is the attack of the incapable fencer.

"By retreating you maintain the distance between yourself and your opponent, and make it difficult for him to get command of your blade on a simulated attack.

"There is only one other movement that I should teach to a novice, who came to me for advice in these circumstances. I should tell him—as he retires and straightens his arm—to change the line occasionally; that is to say to pass his point under his opponent's blade and threaten him on the other side, in fact a simple disengagement. It is the easiest thing in the world to understand, and anyone, however little he may be skilled in the art of fencing, can do it with the greatest ease; the act of retiring itself facilitates the execution of the movement. An hour's practice will make him familiar with this change of line, which as I remarked just now answers the double purpose of attack and defence.

" I should make my pupil repeat this very simple performance over and over again, instructing him to straighten his arm, sometimes with his point held high on a level with the chest, attacking the high lines, sometimes with the point lowered, attacking the low lines. You understand of course what is meant by the high and low lines. It is the A—B—C of fencing.

" Notice that my lesson is simplified to a degree that is almost ludicrous. I dissect every movement and explain how the parts are put together, being particularly careful to avoid the use of technical terms, for my imaginary pupil

is supposed to be completely ignorant, and he
would be hopelessly puzzled by them. If on the
other hand he happens to have some smattering
of knowledge he will appreciate more fully and
derive all the more benefit from the lesson thus
reduced to its simplest expression."

VII.

"You say nothing," remarked one of my
hearers, "about the movement, which consists
in reversing the lunge."

"No," I answered; "because I believe that
this device, which is only proper in certain
exceptional circumstances, is likely to prove
very dangerous if it is employed at the wrong
moment or at random. If it does not come off,
you are left without defence at your opponent's
mercy.

"To put the matter shortly:—if you adopt
my plan, you retire and at the same moment
offer your point either with a straight thrust or
with a disengagement; then you immediately
recover your guard and bring your forearm
back to its original position. Whether your

c.   14

thrust has succeeded or not, you are always provided with a sound defence, you are set firmly on your legs, your balance is undisturbed, and upon your opponent's advance you can repeat the process again and again.

"Now suppose that you decide to lunge to the rear; that is to say, to reverse the lunge by throwing the left leg back to its full extent and dropping the body, without moving the right foot; well, when will you do this and how?

"You are not an expert. What secret instinct will inform you that the opportune moment has come for executing this manoeuvre? For after you have executed it, you must recover, and recover smartly, if you are to regain your guard; no easy matter, I assure you. In attempting to perform a movement so complicated, you with your want of experience can hardly fail to be thrown into disorder, to the great advantage of your adversary, who will seize the opportunity to press you briskly and get command of your blade.

"Even supposing that you escape from this danger, you cannot go on repeating the process continually; you cannot repeat it indifferently on every attack, or on every semblance of an attack that is made upon you. You must judge your opportunity. Now fencing judgment, especially in a duel, implies knowledge, and remember we are arguing on the assumption that you are ignorant.

" For these reasons I should never think of recommending the lunge to the rear to anyone who has not acquired some familiarity with his weapon.

VIII.

" If we now turn from the man whose only chance lies in his getting a rule of thumb to work by to the man who is more or less used to fencing, the case is different. The scope of the lesson is enlarged. The pupil knows a few words of the language, we must try to turn his knowledge to account.

" My advice to him would be :—In the first place, take the same guard as that already indicated ; but make a little play with your point, by changing the line occasionally from inside to outside and so on, in order to bother your opponent. Make a show of attacking now and then, in order to recover any ground that you may have lost by retreating. But be very

careful never on any account to attack in real
earnest. You must be doubly strong and doubly
sure of all your movements to enable you to
attack without getting out of your depth, and
perhaps throwing yourself away in a moment
of inadvertence.

"And then I should go on to say :—Sometimes, but always accompanying the movement
with a short step to the rear, make a parry of
counter quarte and circle, a sweeping parry
which cuts all the lines, and is bound to find
the blade somewhere. Come back to your first
position at once, holding your point well in
front of your body. Then if you find that your
opponent means to develope his attack fully,
and that his point is directed high, throw your
left foot back boldly, remembering to drop your
head and body at the same moment, in order to
avoid the point which would otherwise strike
you in the upper part of the chest or in the
face. Above all, recover as smartly as you can
by springing quickly to the rear, so as to regain
your defensive position before your adversary,
if he has avoided or parried your thrust, can
take advantage of his opportunity.

"But once more I must caution you that
this sort of thing requires such training and

judgment as I should not expect anyone to
possess who has not by regular practice made
himself thoroughly at home with the sword."

IX.

"We are allowed to criticise, I believe,"
remarked the Comte de C. after a pause which
followed these remarks.

"By all means," I replied ; "I not only allow
but invite criticism. In working out an idea,
I may very likely neglect some side of it that
ought not to be passed over."

"Well, you seem to me inconsistent. You
said the other day, and I quite agreed with
you:—'The first and fundamental rule of fencing
is to parry;' and now you tell us on the contrary
not to attempt to parry."

"That is fair criticism," I answered, "but
I do not admit the inconsistency. You will
remember that we were then talking of scientific
fencing, that is to say of the systematic study
of swordsmanship. But that has nothing to do
with the present question. The whole art of
fencing cannot be learnt in three or four hours.

"Let me give you an analogy, for an analogy often serves to put an argument simply. Two men are on a sinking ship; one of them knows how to swim, the other only knows how to go to the bottom and stay there. Meanwhile the danger is immediate. Would you say to the man who cannot swim a stroke:— 'Look here, this is the way to swim; you move your arms like this, and at the same time you move your legs like that'? Do you mean to tell me that he will be able to put into practice straight away what you have just shown him? Or do you suppose, that thanks to your demonstration he will be able to swim when he finds himself in the water? No, of course you are not so foolish as to suppose anything of the sort. You would of course tell him to catch hold of something or other, anything—a spar, an oar, or a plank, and to support himself on it as best he can; that is his only chance.

"Well, my case is on all fours with that. My pupil is in imminent peril of his life. My business is to give him the spar or the plank, which may serve to keep him afloat. I don't bother about teaching him to swim.

X.

"Of course there is nothing to prevent one from showing one or two parries to the novice who has to fight a duel at short notice. But the only parries that would be of any use to him are the comprehensive and rather complicated parries, which sweep through all the lines. What would be the result?

"His parries would be weak, undecided, and slow. Instead of tripping neatly round the blade, they would labour painfully after it in wide circles. To deceive them would be the merest child's play, and the poor novice, encountering nothing but empty air, would let his blade fly into space, and send his arm after it, leaving himself completely exposed.

"Even supposing that his opponent does not take advantage of his opportunity, the novice realises how helpless he is, and racks his brains for some device to avoid the danger when he is again attacked. Then he does not know what to do, what not to do; he loses his head and is seized with panic; he strikes wildly at his opponent's blade, as a drowning man strikes wildly at the water, and nothing remains to be done but to wait for the finishing thrust, or to rush blindly at his opponent, with the probability that he will run upon his point. Those are my reasons for not attempting to teach an untutored novice things which he cannot possibly perform.

"Now, on the other hand, consider in detail the measures that I do put at his disposal. By retiring he evades the point. Evading the point, by drawing the body back or by springing to the rear, may not be the same thing as parrying, but it amounts to much the same in the end, since you retire out of range and are not hit. Or if you are hit, at the worst you can be only lightly touched, because by retiring you make your opponent lose the ground which he reckoned on gaining by his attack.

"Moreover when he sees that you straighten your arm every time on the chance of reaching him, he dare not lunge out recklessly. If he does, you have at least a chance of hitting him,—by a fluke no doubt, but I suppose you do not much mind that.

XI.

"There is one last objection that I will anticipate.

"What, I may be asked, becomes of your scheme of defence, if, the moment that the novice extends his sword at a venture, the adversary engages it?

"Without a doubt that is what he ought to do, and what he will do, as I shall presently explain. But you do not imagine, I suppose, that a man completely ignorant of the use of his weapon, who goes to a professor for advice on the eve of an encounter, can hope to come away comforted with the assurance that he has learnt the whole art of how to hit his opponent without being touched himself? That, I fancy, would be too convenient. It would be better then to study the art of not learning to fence, instead of spending months and years in studying the art of fencing. Ignorance would indeed be bliss and wisdom folly.

"The man who has not learnt the use of the weapon to which he entrusts his life, may think himself lucky if he can lessen the chances, to which he is exposed, of a fatal issue. The master can hope to accomplish nothing more than to give his pupil some confidence, and show him the only course that can be commended by common sense and at the same time furnishes some sort of defence.

"If the novice does what he is told he will, I repeat, put difficulties and dangers in the way of his opponent; he will force him to act with caution, he will keep him at long range, and compel him to shift his ground when he attacks. In shifting his ground he may, either through carelessness or in the excitement of the moment, leave himself uncovered, and give an opening to the point that is continually directed at him. But I do not for a moment suppose that a wary and experienced fencer, who keeps his head cool, will not easily defeat such elementary strategy.

"You may tell your pupil to be prudent, you may tell him to be calm and resolute, but now or never you should add the pious wish 'Heaven help you'."

XII.

"May I ask one more question?" said one of my friends. "I have often heard it said that if you don't know much about fencing the best thing to do is, as soon as you come on guard, to make a sudden rush at the other man before he has time to collect himself."

"Well," I replied, "if you wish to make sure of being incurably spitted, that is the most infallible way to set about it.

"The seconds, before giving the signal to begin, have just asked your opponent if he is ready. Is it likely that he will allow himself to be rushed, or to be victimised by such a transparent piece of bluff?

"Is it not much more likely that he will have been told to look out for a surprise attack? One of two things,—either the man who confronts you is a skilful fencer, in which case he will not want you to give him time to collect himself, but will be quite capable of taking his own time; or his ignorance of fencing is on a par with yours, and then it is a toss up. It follows that if this desperate plan of attack is chosen, because it is thought likely to succeed, it is absurd. If however it is chosen, because the man who chooses it is of a restive impatient disposition, one who cannot wait and for whom cool defensive tactics are an impossibility, the case is different.

"All that one can say to the pupil, whose temper is such that he cannot play a waiting game, is something of this sort :—Trust your instinct, be guided by your natural impulse. You quite understand that by acting as you propose you run a greater risk ; for your attack is delivered at random, you are embarking on a wild and hazardous speculation. Your only chance of success, as you yourself admit, is that you may, by suddenly and violently letting yourself go for all you are worth, take your opponent by surprise and put him off his parry. I can only give you one word of advice. Before letting yourself go, try at any rate to beat the other man's sword out of line in any way you can. Knock it up or down, to one side or the other ; as soon as you have made your beat, let yourself go straight, without the least hesitation. By this means you will avoid an interchange of hits or a

stop thrust.   But I warn you this is not so easy
as it sounds.

"Possibly, where so much depends on luck
and accident, you may bring off your hit.   But if
you are the wounded man, you will be wounded
with a vengeance, for you will probably run on
the sword up to the hilt,—a trifling consideration,
which is perhaps worth taking into account.

"This plan in fact can never be recom-
mended ; it involves not only too many risks,
but risks that are too serious and too certain.
I will show you presently in greater detail why
this is so, when we look at the question from the
other side, from the point of view of a fencer
more or less skilful, who is opposed to a novice
ignorant of swordsmanship but a determined
natural fighter, who is thoroughly roused by a
keen sense of danger.

XIII.

"The case we shall consider next will be the
reverse of this.   By reversing the position we
shall hear what is to be said on both sides, and
we shall then have considered from every point

of view, the probabilities of victory or defeat,
which are likely to occur in a duel. We will
leave that for to-morrow."

And so we broke up.

The Eleventh Evening

The real thing.

I.

" WE have now to examine the duel with swords from a different point of view. The ignorant and inexperienced fencer, trying at the last moment to find a desperate remedy for a desperate state of affairs, may be dismissed, and we have now to consider the case of combatants who are more or less evenly matched, and who are fighting in deadly earnest. For as I have already said, a duel generally equalises the forces on either side, except when a skilful and resolute swordsman meets a clumsy hesitating duffer, or

when a cool head is opposed to that rash and
furious bluster which more often than not leads
a man to his destruction.

"First and foremost, your invariable rule
must be :—Distrust your enemy ; never be over-
confident. I cannot too often repeat that the
unexpected always turns up just when you are
least prepared for it. It is this glorious uncertainty that to my mind makes fighting with
swords the only sort of duelling that is fair and
sportsmanlike, the only sort in which energy,
courage, and resolution always give some chance
to the weaker combatant.

"In a duel fought with pistols, what a
wretched rôle is assigned to the combatants.
Energy is of no use, courage of no value ; you
stand up like a target to be shot at, without any
possibility of defence. Courage and cowardice
meet on equal terms ; the feeblest and most
spiritless sneak may succeed in defeating the
most determined courage and the manliest
energy. A finger presses a trigger, and the
thing is done. Duelling with pistols has always
seemed to me a monstrous practice. I am delighted to see it disappearing from our manners,
and going more and more out of fashion every
day.

II.

"To return to my subject,—there are certain elementary principles of self-defence, from which the prudent fencer ought never to depart ; principles of such universal application, that they may be considered the foundation on which is based all serious fighting, which is conducted with any sort of method.

"As soon as the second who undertakes to start the proceedings has put you on guard, and steps back, leaving you at liberty to set to, you should immediately take two or three paces to the rear, before your opponent can realise or anticipate what you are about. By this means you at once put yourself out of range, and out of danger either from a surprise or from one of those blind and frantic rushes, to which, as we have seen, some men are apt to pin their faith."

"But," exclaimed one of my hearers, not altogether seriously, "if your opponent does the same thing, you will find yourselves at a range more suitable for pistol practice than for sword-play."

"In that case," I replied, taking him seriously, "you have three advantages for one,— surely a substantial gain.

"In the first place, if the same idea has occurred to your opponent as to you, or if the same advice has been given to you both, the advice is the more likely to be sound.

"In the second place, his quick strategic movement to the rear tells you very plainly that he too has no fancy for a surprise, or for that rough and tumble style of fighting which reduces sword-play to a sort of fisticuffs. You are able to make up your mind at once that he is not that sort of fighter, and that his attacks will be prudent and well considered.

"In the third place, the brief pause gives you a moment or two to pull yourself together and get steady, to take a good look at your opponent's point, and get over that first involuntary sensation, that momentary chill, which no one, not even the bravest of us, ever fails to experience. It also gives you time to run your eye over your antagonist, and by noting how he stands, how he holds his sword, in a word how he shapes, to look the situation in the face and settle your plan of campaign.

"That, I think you will admit, is something gained, even if you have to stand for a few seconds at a range which, as you say, seems more suitable for pistol practice.

III.

"Have you never observed how all animals, from the most insignificant creatures up to the most savage beasts, set about fighting? Look at two cocks in a back-yard or two bulls in a field. Notice how they skirmish and spar before really letting themselves go ; notice the wicked glitter of their eyes as they intently watch for an opening, where they will presently plant their most telling blow.

"What teaches them not to rush at each other's throat in blind fury? Why, simply instinct, the science of self-preservation which is common to every living thing ; and common instinct should teach you the same lesson.

"You will easily realise how completely you upset or at least disturb the calculations of the man who is clinging to advice of this kind :—
'The moment you are on guard,—lunge, before

your opponent has time to collect himself'; or of the man, whose one idea is to make a wild and indiscriminate charge.

"Such men, however lacking they may be in brains, can hardly fail to perceive that the distance between you and them makes a surprise impracticable. If they do attempt it, their movements will be disconcerted; they will give themselves away, and may probably run upon your point if you hold it straight before you, or in any case they must give you time to see them coming. You may be attacked no doubt, and attacked furiously, but you will not be surprised.

IV.

"When you have placed yourself out of range you remain free to choose your next move. If your opponent now seems inclined to shorten the distance between you, wait for him without breaking ground. He is compelled to advance, and therefore is at a disadvantage; for if he exposes himself, you are ready for him; you do your best to harass his advance, you watch your opportunity, and whatever movement he makes you let him see that he is continually threatened by your point.   He cannot help giving you notice of his attack ; you see what is coming, and are able to take your measures accordingly.   The way he manages his advance, and the accompanying movements of his point, hand, and arm, are sure signs by which you can tell how much or how little he knows.

"If on the other hand he stands on the defensive and seems inclined to wait for your attack, you may advance cautiously, with short steps, keeping your legs well under you and your body well balanced, levelling your point now at his eyes, now at his chest ;—for you must be careful to guard against the dangers that I have just mentioned.

"In order to counteract, or at least to lessen the disadvantage to which you are exposed on your advance, you must occupy your opponent's attention by continually threatening him in the different lines ; for by compelling him to protect himself you prevent him from attacking you, and meanwhile little by little you gain ground.

"It is a good plan to feint a serious attack in order to compel him to show his hand, and to find out whether he means to rely on a parry, or if he will simply straighten his arm.   But you

must be very sure of yourself, and have complete
control of your movements, or you will very
likely disclose your own plans by some involuntary and incautious gesture.

"All that I have said applies with equal
force to good and bad fencers, to the expert as
well as to the novice. Prudence and self-control
are more than half the battle. To these must
be added science, which enables you to deceive
your opponent by deluding him as to your real
object, while you compel him unwillingly to
betray himself.

V.

"I hope," I said, interrupting myself, "that
you find me tolerably intelligible and that you
follow the connection between the successive
steps of my argument?"

My audience with one voice assured me that
I was perfectly intelligible, and that they were
following me with the greatest interest.

"I may be a trifle long-winded in dealing
with these points, but please remember that
after pointing out a danger or giving a piece
of advice, I have to show how the danger may
be met, by explaining the answering move.

"To proceed,—whichever of you has made the first advance, you are now within striking distance.

"If you are absolutely ignorant of sword-play, like the unfortunate duellist whose case we were considering last night, I have already told you what in my opinion you can do, or at least may attempt to do. I have nothing more to say on that head.

"The opponents that we now have in view are supposed to have a knowledge of the use of weapons. It follows that the questions to be considered will naturally resemble those that we have already discussed when talking of theoretical sword-play and more particularly of the assault. The only difference is the difference between a sham fight and a real fight, the difference between a muzzled foil and an unmuzzled sword. Besides that, in an assault you are governed by conventional restrictions clearly defined and well understood ; you do not attempt to hit your opponent except in accordance with the rules ; you wear a mask and a jacket.

"But the mistakes which you are most anxious to avoid in an assault are the very things that you try to turn to account in a fight, in order to perplex your opponent and spoil his game. For fencing, if the professors will allow me to say so, is perhaps the one art in which mistakes may upon occasion prove of the greatest possible advantage to him who makes them. Otherwise it would be mere bookwork, to be learnt more or less thoroughly, and the man who knew his book completely would have nothing to fear; but to my mind it is nothing of the sort. No knowledge of fencing can make a man invulnerable. If anyone imagines that he is an exception to the rule he betrays a singularly misplaced confidence in his own powers,—a very dangerous error.

"But ought we to condemn swordsmanship on that account? My own opinion is that this uncertainty is the great beauty of the sword, the one feature that distinguishes it as the only weapon for a fair fight; for even the weakest player has his opportunity, his lucky moments, his strokes of fortune, which must always prevent the duel from degenerating into simple butchery.

"If fencing were an exact science, if you knew, that as sure as two and two make four, you could certainly hit your man, and that he as certainly could not hit you, how could you in common honesty cross swords with him?

VI.

"I am afraid that I have been wandering somewhat from my text; but this digression, though it may at first sight seem out of place, still when one comes to consider it is very closely connected with our subject. For it serves to emphasise once more the fact that, in spite of every probability, luck may always turn the scale in favour of the other side, and to remind you that you cannot attach too much importance to the most minute particulars of your defence.

"Habitual mistrust is one of the most necessary requirements for this complicated art. Put in another way it is the careful study of the enemy whom you have to face. The mistrust that marks the wary, calculating player, not only preserves him from danger but creates dangers for his opponent.

VII.

"I was saying the other day that I did not believe in secret thrusts, and that the thrusts that have received this absurd misnomer are nothing but strokes that are not generally re-cognised by the ordinary rules of fencing. Strip them of their imaginary terrors, and far from being dangerous to you they become more than a little dangerous for the man who attempts them.

"To describe them, we need not distinguish more than two sorts,—methods of attack, and methods of evading or dodging an opponent's attack. These tricks are all very much of the same character. Take this for an example: —lunge as though you were making a simple attack, then suddenly draw your arm back to make your opponent parry in the air, throw yourself out of line and let drive, hitting him in the ribs.

"Or again :—after a false attack, dodge by stooping low to avoid the parry and riposte, and hit your opponent in the low lines. The sudden disappearance of your body will probably as-tonish him.

"Some men delight in charging at you with a shout, at the same time drawing back their arm to avoid your parry. This strange war-cry occasionally has the effect of causing a moment's involuntary pause, of which they take advantage to drive their point home anyhow and anywhere.

"Others again, when the blades are engaged in tierce, suddenly bring their left foot to the front, at the same time swinging the body round, left shoulder forward and out of line with your point.

"If on the other hand these strokes, which if not foul are decidedly irregular, are employed to meet an attack, the same thing is done with slight variations. Suppose I deliver an attack ; my opponent, instead of parrying, springs aside out of line. Sword and body vanish ; the target has moved away ; my attack loses itself in space, and I am hit by a flank movement.

"Or again, he ducks suddenly, supporting himself on his free hand, and allows my point to pass harmlessly over his head, while at the same time he hits me somewhere,—in the low lines of course.

"Or again, he seizes my blade in tierce, swings the left foot round to the front, suddenly arrives at close quarters, and before I have time either to retreat or to recover my guard, stabs me by drawing back or dropping his hand.

"I might extend this list of examples indefinitely, but you see that all these strokes are contrived on the same plan, and only differ from each other in unimportant details. It needs no argument to prove how completely the man who resorts to such tactics gives himself away if they are unsuccessful, for in order to make them really formidable there must be no hanging back,—you must let yourself go without the least reserve."

VIII.

"But surely," someone objected, "in the hands of a skilful swordsman they would be doubly dangerous?"

"That contingency," I replied, " is worth considering, but a skilful swordsman would be very unlikely to resort to such methods. Why should he? If his opponent is a duffer, he has no need to be so tricky. If on the other hand his opponent is a cool-headed fencer, as skilful as himself, he knows the penalty of failure too well to make the attempt.

"I need hardly tell you,—though I believe I have mentioned the fact already,—that when you attack you ought to be particularly careful not to let yourself go so completely that you cannot recover your defensive position, if your attack fails.

"All these remarks illustrate how necessary it is to distrust your enemy, to approach a strange antagonist with caution, and always keep him at a distance. By retreating the moment you come on guard you have already provided against a surprise and against wild rushes. When you are within range, take my advice and do not join blades, and always, as much as possible, avoid coming to such close quarters that your opponent can reach you without breaking ground. But do not misunderstand me when I tell you not to join blades. I do not mean that you are never to cover yourself, and never to allow the blades to meet ; that would be a mistake. All that I mean is that you should take care never to allow your opponent to hold your blade. By playing light and refusing a proffered engagement you put a stop to all forcing strokes,—*croisés*, beats, binds, *flancon-nade,*—which are the most dangerous of all strokes, because they are the most certain. I call them certain, because by holding your blade prisoner they control it forcibly, and make a stop thrust or an exchange of hits impossible.

IX.

" There are of course several ways of dealing with a man who refuses to engage, but they are difficult and require much practice. It generally happens that your refusal disconcerts your opponent. He has no definite point to start from, he hesitates, and his hesitation retards his attack.

" If his attack is complicated, you may venture on a stop thrust, offered with caution and accompanied by a short step to the rear; and you worry, and annoy, and wear him out to the best of your ability.

" If his attack is simple, he will be afraid of an exchange of hits; and the more skilful he is, the more cautious you will find him ; and as I said when speaking of the assault, you may lessen the danger of a simple attack by a brisk retreat to a greater or less distance, as the case may be. By this means you parry more easily, you increase the distance to be traversed, and you counteract the rapidity of the attack by two methods of defence instead of one.

" If you are hit, the wound is slight, or at

all events much less severe than it would have been, if you had tried to parry without breaking ground. If on the other hand your parry is successful, you have escaped the danger of a *corps à corps*, and are in a better position for delivering your riposte.

" So much for the defence, now let us suppose that you are the attacking party. You attack, either because you place more reliance on the quickness of your hand than on the certainty of your riposte, or because your opponent, by confining himself to defensive tactics, compels you to do so. You must be doubly cautious now.

X.

"If it is important, as I have just now pointed out, to avoid engaging blades when you are acting on the defensive, in order to protect yourself from what may be called attacks on the sword, it is obviously of equal importance never to attack without first attempting to master your opponent's *fort*.

" Eschew feints ;—I have shown you how dangerous they are—therefore be content with direct attacks, prefacing them with an engagement in *carte* or *tierce*, or with a pressure, or a beat, light or heavy, accordingly as you wish to draw your opponent to one line or another. Your object will be gained more easily, if he is willing to join blades.

"If on the other hand he is unwilling to do so, you must by force or fraud bring him to an engagement, and you should never finish your attack until you have succeeded in finding his blade; unless in his efforts to elude you he leaves himself completely exposed. When that happens a straight thrust is a certainty.

"What you have most to fear is a stop thrust, the straightening of your opponent's arm on your preparation or advance. This is generally a favourite stroke with those who deliberately stand on the defensive.

"In nine cases out of ten the refusal to join blades may be successfully met by a simulated attack, if it is well marked. Either your opponent attempts to parry, or he straightens his arm; whereupon you immediately engage his blade, and drive your attack home, without quitting his blade, and above all without any feint.

XI.

" It is evidently impossible to enumerate in the course of conversation all the situations that may occur, or to describe all the traps that you may set for your opponent or that he may set for you. These things are matters of instinct and inspiration, the happy thoughts of the moment, and depend on character and individual temperament, physical and moral. The art of fighting cannot of course be learnt in a day ; it grows upon you gradually, as you learn by experience to combine the various elements scientifically into a well-ordered whole.

" Picture for yourselves two men fighting.— You see them at one moment standing their full height, the next bent double, swerving to right and left, colliding violently, and entangled in a furious encounter ; suddenly they break away, recoiling from each other with a bound, rest for a moment, panting and glaring, till suddenly they renew the struggle. Do you suppose that all these intricate evolutions, and the subtle application of muscular force that they imply, can be systematically analysed and taught ? Of course not.

"In every art proficiency can only be obtained by persistent and intelligent application. Practice alone makes perfect. It is by studying combinations, by trying to adapt the means at his disposal to the object in view, that the artist tests the limits of his art and discovers its hidden secrets, fashions it at will, and makes it his obedient slave.

"These remarks would not be complete, if I failed to caution you against a very pernicious habit, which one is apt to contract in the fencing-room, and which in a duel may easily lead to a fatal issue. I mean the habit of stopping after you have made a hit, instead of immediately recovering your guard and putting yourself out of distance. Never forget this important point; if you do, you may after wounding your opponent receive a mortal wound, for which you will have only yourself to blame.

"Every fencer knows how commonly it happens in an assault, that a man ripostes automatically after he is hit, and strikes his opponent almost simultaneously, especially when the latter has not taken the trouble to attend strictly to his recovery.

"Remember that a sword-thrust, even though

it be mortal, does not take effect immediately. There is always a momentary interval before the wounded man falters, or drops his sword, or falls to the ground unconscious. The moment you think you have made a hit,—for you may be mistaken,—get back as smartly as you can, and be ready to go on fighting.

XII.

"Well," I added after a short pause, "nothing else occurs to me in the way of general advice, which I can commend to your notice. When the time for actual fighting arrives, your attention must be concentrated on the important points, and these may be summed up in two or three words :—self-reliance, well-judged caution, restrained and well-timed energy."

"You have given us most excellent advice," exclaimed the Comte de C. "If one could only think of it all at the critical moment, one would be well provided."

"Think of only half of it," I answered, "and you will not do so badly,—there are so many men who cannot think at all."

XIII.

The next day we all met as usual in the smoking-room.

"Well," someone asked me, "what are you going to talk about to-night?"

"Why," I answered, "my subject is exhausted, I have told you all I know, or at any rate all that I think worth knowing."

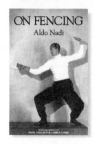

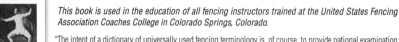